SESSIONS WITH THESSALONIANS

Smyth & Helwys Publishing, Inc.
6316 Peake Road
Macon, Georgia 31210-3960
1-800-747-3016
© 2007 by Smyth & Helwys Publishing
All rights reserved.
Printed in the United States of America.

The paper used in this publication meets the minimum
requirements of American National Standard for Information
Sciences—Permanence of Paper for Printed Library Materials.

Library of Congress Cataloging-in-Publication Data

Letson, Rickey.
Sessions with Thessalonians : being faithful in a confusing world /
by Rickey Letson.
p. cm.
Includes bibliographical references.
ISBN 978-1-57312-491-1 (pbk. : alk. paper)
1. Bible. N.T. Thessalonians—Criticism, interpretation, etc.
2. Bible. N.T. Thessalonians—Textbooks. I. Title.

BS2725.52.L48 2007
227'.810071—dc22

2007015202

Sessions *with*
Thessalonians

● ● ● Being *Faithful* in a
Confusing World

Rickey Letson

SMYTH&HELWYS
PUBLISHING, INCORPORATED · MACON, GEORGIA

Dedication

To Ann Marie and Callie, the most important ladies in my life, who patiently provided me with time to write and who encouraged me every step of the way. I love you both!

To my dad and mom, Don and Deborah Letson, who always believe in me, even when I doubt myself. No one could have finer parents.

To the congregations at Moulton, Dawson Memorial, Castalia, Lindley Park, Immanuel, and Johns Creek, who have formed my faith and enriched my life.

Special thanks to Michael McCullar for countless hours of help in editing and for his invaluable suggestions and guidance in the preparation of the final manuscript.

Table of Contents

Sessions with Thessalonians

Sessions with Thessalonians is a ten-session guide designed for use by individuals or groups. The goal of this resource is to provide a solid biblical, contextual, and theological overview of the two letters of the New Testament to which we refer as 1 and 2 Thessalonians. These letters provide us with insights into some of the basic characteristics necessary for both ancient and modern believers to truly live out their faith in the world around them.

The subtitle of this volume in the Sessions Series is *Being Faithful in a Confusing World*. This phrase is meant to convey a couple of distinct thoughts about the two letters to the believers in Thessalonica. First, as new believers, the Thessalonians had a difficult time understanding what it meant to follow Christ faithfully. Questions regarding issues such as suffering, the second coming, death, and discipline were abundant within this young, small congregation trying to find its way. They had entered a confusing new world and were in great need of Paul's navigational abilities.

Second, attempting to live as a follower of Christ within the culture of Thessalonica was filled with numerous difficulties. The Thessalonians felt overwhelmed by the persecution they were enduring. They struggled with implementing sexual ethics in a culture where there were none. And they were perplexed by how one lives each day with the tension of the imminent return of Jesus. Like us, they wrestled daily with keeping their faith alive in a world often opposed to the very message their lives were now built around.

I have studied, reflected upon, and wrestled with these two magnificent letters for many months now. As a result, it has become my deep conviction that Paul's words to the Thessalonians in the midst of their confusion remain invaluable words for believers today who live in a world that is just as chaotic. I trust and pray that you will adopt the same sentiments as you make your way through the pages of this book and as you read closely each line of the Thessalonian writings. Indeed, we are all better off since these love letters from Paul to the Thessalonians also found safe passage to each of us.

Resource Pages

Each chapter of *Sessions with Thessalonians* ends with questions meant to spur further thinking and discussion. The intent is that these pages will provide the reader with further insight into the connection between Paul's letters and modernity. These questions are provided in order to be useful either to an individual for private study and personal development or to a group that may use them as good places to begin discussion and conversation about the text.

Rickey Letson
Advent 2006

Introducing 1 and 2 Thessalonians

Before moving into a detailed look at these two letters, it is important to gather broad information about the sender, recipients, date of composition, and reason for the writings. This knowledge will be critical in our attempt to interpret properly and fully appreciate these texts.

The Sender

Paul, the great apostle and preeminent New Testament missionary, is often named as the sender of thirteen letters that eventually made their way into the New Testament. Throughout the centuries, 1 and 2 Thessalonians have consistently been included in this list. Pauline scholars, however, have long suggested that among the thirteen letters connected with Paul, only seven seem to have unequivocally come from the pen of the infamous apostle. These seven commonly include Galatians, Romans, 1 and 2 Corinthians, Philippians, Philemon, and 1 Thessalonians. This group exhibits a similar theology, vocabulary, and syntax in keeping with what we know of Paul. Likewise, these letters can easily be connected to the historical travels of Paul as laid out by the book of Acts, where we find our most extensive account of Paul's life.

The other six New Testament writings connected to Paul all possess various characteristics that call into question the possibility that he was actually their author. This group includes Ephesians, Colossians, 1 and 2 Timothy, Titus, and 2 Thessalonians. In these letters, the vocabulary, grammatical style, and at times theology seem different from what we find in the aforementioned seven letters. So too, as seen most explicitly in 1 and 2 Timothy and Titus, which we call the Pastoral Epistles, the author sometimes seems to address a period in the church's history after the lifetime of Paul.

In the case of 2 Thessalonians, the argument against Paul as the author seems to hinge on two points. First, there is the sense that the second letter appears to be repetitious of the first letter at several points. Second, scholars voice a concern that 2 Thessalonians 1 contradicts the viewpoint of 1 Thessalonians 4 and 5 in regard to the perspectives of the second coming in both letters. By far the most troubling issue is the second letter and the apparent contradictions related to Christ's return.

In 1 Thessalonians 4 and 5, Paul is adamant that Christ will return like "a thief in the night" (5:2). His emphasis is that the return will be sudden and without warning. However, in 2 Thessalonians 1, the author takes great pains to talk about the second coming in light of events that will clearly signal Christ's arrival. In other words, 1 Thessalonians appears to advocate an attitude that Christ's return cannot be predicted by world events, while 2 Thessalonians seems just as bent on the idea that definite signs will indicate that the return is close at hand. How could the same person have written both perspectives?

At the same time, it should be noted that there are many in the scholarly community who continue to favor Paul as author of 2 Thessalonians. When posed with the concerns mentioned, they generally respond by arguing that in 2 Thessalonians, Paul is merely developing further his thoughts and beliefs, which solves the redundancy issue. Likewise, in terms of the suggested contradiction regarding the second coming, they respond by offering the plausible perspective that the two letters actually complement one another, suggesting that in 2 Thessalonians, Paul says that while the return of Christ will definitely catch most off guard and be like a "thief," there are still signs to watch for and to note.

In this book, I will speak of Paul when referring to the sender of 2 Thessalonians. This is *not* meant to affirm that Paul was definitely the author of the letter. Rather, it is merely a way to provide continuity within this look at the two letters.

The Recipients

Thessalonica was an interesting place to say the least. Situated on the Egnatian Road and a major port city, Thessalonica was at the heart of commerce in the ancient world as trade flowed between Rome and the East. Thessalonica was also the capital of the

Macedonian Province within the Roman Empire and therefore a significant part of the governmental process. Suffice it to say, Thessalonica was a bustling city where important business took place and through which interesting characters from all over the empire passed.

According to Acts 17, the church at Thessalonica appears to have come to be as a result of the three weeks Paul spent preaching there in the city synagogue. After that period, the believers appear to have moved their meeting point to the home of Jason, an apparently wealthy Thessalonian citizen and one of Paul's early converts in the city.

How long Paul remained in Thessalonica is uncertain. A strict reading of Acts 17 has led some to the assumption that Paul was only in the city for three weeks before being run out of town by the local officials. Others suggest that this text from Acts merely points out that Paul preached in the synagogue for three weeks. He likely spent further time there plying his trade and sharing about Christ during his daily labors as a tentmaker. This view can be supported by Paul's own words in 1 Thessalonians 2:9ff.

Either way, it appears all but certain that Paul's stay in the city was a short one. Rather quickly, be it after three weeks or a few months, the authorities ran Paul out of the city and he and his fellow missionaries headed west. Obviously, this left the young Thessalonians in a fragile state. New in their faith and already being persecuted by their fellow citizens, it is no wonder that their safety and the perseverance of their faith and congregation concerned Paul.

One other thing should be noted about the Thessalonian context. Like many of the other sites of early Christian congregations, Thessalonica was home to numerous other gods from both the citizens' Greek heritage and Roman rule. Evidence suggests that the Thessalonian citizens, like others within the empire, also worshipped the Roman emperor and considered him to be a god. (Blevins, 909-10)

Among the Thessalonian pantheon was an interesting figure called Cabirus. The cult of Cabirus was centered in Macedonia and Thrace. It focused on a legendary young man who was murdered by his two brothers. It was said that Cabirus would return one day to aid the powerless of the city. His symbol was the hammer, and he easily became associated with and worshipped by the working class in Thessalonica. Although no one knows why, at some point the

Cabirus cult was taken over by the ruling elite and included in the official cult. Since it was common belief in those days that the gods listened more attentively to the wealthy than to the poor, the powerless of Thessalonica felt as though their hope had been taken from them.

In the light of the Cabirus cult, it is easy to understand how Paul's preaching of Jesus could have easily gained traction in Thessalonica. After all, Jesus himself, like Cabirus, was a young man wrongly murdered who had indeed risen from the dead to bring good news to the poor and downtrodden. (Murphy-O'Connor, 74-75)

Date of Composition

Many biblical scholars consider the Thessalonian correspondence to be our oldest writings in the New Testament. The sense is that Paul sent Timothy back to Thessalonica shortly after the initial visit there in order to check on the congregation. When Timothy returned with his report, Paul appears to have decided to write to the congregation in order to encourage them further and to deal with questions and issues raised to Timothy during his return visit. The best guess is that Paul wrote 1 Thessalonians while in Corinth around AD 50 only a few months after the original visit. Many feel that 2 Thessalonians followed shortly afterward and that it was likely composed in Corinth too. (Blevins, 909)

It is also interesting to note that no one knows for certain that 1 Thessalonians was written first and 2 Thessalonians second. While this is a good possibility, when the New Testament books were put together, correspondence to the same congregation was simply ordered from longest to shortest with the longest letter being labeled as "first" and so forth in descending order. (Efird, 105)

Reason for Writing

As with all biblical books, numerous themes are addressed over the course of the chapters and verses of the two letters to which we refer as 1 and 2 Thessalonians. Three overarching issues, however, seem to be at the center of the correspondence and provide at least partial basis for a majority of the sessions within this book. These three aspects are at the heart of what Paul had to say.

Encouragement. Due to reports he was obviously receiving from the church at Thessalonica, Paul wanted to encourage the young believers and infant congregation to stay committed to Christ and their newfound faith. It is evident that in light of their apparent persecution, Paul felt that he needed to help his friends in the Thessalonian church to know he loved them, supported them, and was proud of the great strides they were making for the gospel's sake. Paul longed to visit Thessalonica, but, if a personal visit was not a possibility, Paul chose the only other means available for expressing his feelings—a personal letter.

In this same vein, Paul also wanted the Thessalonians to understand that he was encouraged by their hard work and the obvious fruits of their faith. Not all of the early Pauline congregations had faired as well as the Thessalonians. Not all of Paul's teachings had been received as heartily or put into practice so faithfully. This reality meant that just as Paul wanted to encourage the Thessalonians, he also wanted them to know that the faith and practice they exhibited on a daily basis encouraged him. Through them, he had been reminded that his work was not in vain and that at least in some places it was most definitely taking root.

Sacrifice. Not only were the Thessalonians being persecuted for the faith, but they were also confused as to what this persecution signified. Evidently, many in the church feared that the difficulties befalling them signified that their faith was deficient. In other words, persecution signified a faith riddled with problems that needed attention.

In these letters, Paul takes great pains to communicate to the Thessalonians that nothing could be further from the truth. Paul desperately wanted them to recognize that suffering and sacrifice as a result of Christ was a sure sign that one's faith was vibrant, healthy, and alive. To suffer was merely a part of discipleship. When there was no suffering, this was the point at which one should question the health and well-being of their spiritual walk, not vice versa.

Questions Regarding the End. The apocalyptic strand within Judaism influenced Paul. This meant that part of his Jewish heritage was the belief that the coming of the Messiah would also signal the end of the age. After the Damascus Road experience, Paul simply imported this belief into his faith in Christ. In short, his acceptance of Christ as Messiah meant that he also now believed the end of time was right around the corner and would certainly occur within his lifetime. Therefore, when Paul ushered in the church planter movement, he offered these teachings about the impending end of the age as a bedrock of proper theology (Ehrman, 118-19).

After Paul had moved on from Thessalonica to other places of ministry, the congregation left behind began to have numerous questions about this aspect of their beliefs. After all, days were stretching into months and years and they were still around. Likewise, members of the church were dying and countless uncertainties loomed as to how the deceased figured into the end of all things. There was even the suggestion present that the return of Christ had already taken place. Further still, it appears that members of the church were using the impending end as a reason to sit around waiting and watching the skies rather than working and contributing to the well-being of the body.

Paul's reflections on the end of all things are included in both letters. His comments attempt to address the numerous issues swirling within the Thessalonian community. In relatively short space, Paul provides guidance on waiting and watching for the return, perspective regarding those who have died and how they will figure into the end, a dismissal of the notion that the end had already occurred, and sharp criticism of those who appear to be using Christ's imminent return as an excuse for living as first-century freeloaders by not working. Interestingly, Paul's response to the Thessalonians regarding end times was not only valuable guidance for early believers, but these words also continue to shape our own theology of the end. In fact, these two letters provide some of the longest and most direct teaching within the entire New Testament on the subject.

Live Caring for Others—
Encouragement

Session   *1 Thessalonians 1:1-10; 3:6-10*

Central Truth of the Session

Everyone faces moments in which they wonder if their actions are worth the cost. When such moments occur, it is important for others to come along who can champion our cause, pat us on the back, and whisper into our ears that our sacrifices are not in vain. The encouragement of others plays a pivotal role in our ability to fight the good fight, especially when connected to matters of faith.

The Intersection of Thessalonians and Today

Imagine that, feeling called by God, you have chosen to take a year's leave of absence from your job. Along with your family, you feel led to go to a remote part of the world to share the love of Christ with a group of people that have yet to hear about Jesus. You store your valuables, lock up the house, make provisions for the children to continue their education in a remote setting, jump through all of the hoops and mounds of paperwork at the office, and say good-bye to family and friends.

As expected, the adjustments to the new setting are extremely difficult, complete with strange food, an unusual climate, rodents of unusual sizes (think *The Princess Bride*), and harsh living conditions. Amazingly, though, the people accept you and your family quickly and lovingly. Within a matter of only a few weeks, numerous folks in the community have already accepted your teachings about Jesus and have started to believe. A small group has even begun to meet with you in your home for study and prayer.

At this moment, when things appear as though they couldn't possibly go any better, disaster strikes. Some within the community who are not quite as hospitable begin to question your motives and suggest that you and your family are actually poisoning people's minds. They say you are power hungry and you will ultimately use your so-called religion for the purpose of manipulation and control. Their rhetoric turns to anger and subsequent threats of violence. Before long, you realize that the survival of your family depends on abandoning the mission and returning home as soon as possible.

Back home, numerous thoughts literally flood your mind. Should you have left? How are those infants in the faith who accepted Christ before you left now doing? Could they and their faith possibly survive without the presence of your family? Were the emotional scares, trauma, and sacrifices of the experience worth the limited results and short stay? Having left a community with no phones or e-mail and little contact with the outside world, what if anything can you do to support and help your friends there now?

The Thessalonian Context

Paul, Silas, and Timothy, along with the early believers in Thessalonica, found themselves immersed in a situation similar to the one just described. As was mentioned in the introduction, the stay of Paul and his colleagues in Thessalonica was both successful and short. While many quickly accepted and trusted in what the three missionaries had to say, numerous other Thessalonian citizens called for the dismissal of the three from their city. Whether Paul, Silas, and Timothy were in Thessalonica for only three Sabbaths as Acts suggests (see Acts 17:2), or for a little longer as some biblical scholars argue, the group's stay in the city was short at best.

All too quickly, hostilities in Thessalonica forced the three to move on down the Egnation Road to some other locale that might be more hospitable. As they went, one can assume that the dusty roadside was watered with their tears of love and concern for the small group of believers being left behind. Certainly the survival of the infant Christians in Thessalonica was questionable.

At some point after their hasty exit from Thessalonica, Timothy was able to make his way back to the city in order to visit with the young believers there. When Timothy returned to Paul and Silas after his visit, he had learned among other things two important truths: the believers in Thessalonica had continued in their faith, and opponents within the city had continued their persecution of the group.

This persecution is not surprising for at least two reasons. First, as is clear from 1:9, the Thessalonian believers had "turned to God from idols" (NRSV). Idolatry of all sorts, including worship of the Roman emperor, was common within Thessalonica at that time. In fact, it was so much a part of normal everyday life that the Thessalonian believers would have been seen as abnormal by abstaining from such behavior. The reality that idol worship was a major part of both public life as well as a major underpinning of the social society of the time meant that the Thessalonian believers stood out like a sore thumb in almost every possible setting.

Second, it is also significant to recognize that the Thessalonians had not simply turned away from the gods of the day; they had also turned toward worship of Jesus. For most people of that time, if Jesus was remembered at all, it was as a crazed, Jewish peasant who had attempted to overthrow the Roman government. They knew that his so-called rebellion had been quickly quashed and that his life had ended rather abruptly when the Romans executed him (DeSilva, 27-28). That the Thessalonian believers had turned from the accepted religious practices of the day in order to worship this kind of questionable character should leave little doubt as to why they were persecuted and treated so viciously.

Paul's Words of Encouragement to the Thessalonians (1 Thess 1:1-10)

In spite of the persecution, word reached Paul that the Thessalonians were well. Obviously, Paul recognized that the faithfulness of the Thessalonians was no small accomplishment. It appears that he also understood that similar faithfulness would be required if the Thessalonians were to continue to grow and mature in spite of the daily obstacles they faced. In light of all of this, Paul chose to do the only thing one could do. He responded to the good report from Timothy by writing a letter to the Thessalonians. As we shall see, this letter is multifaceted. But, if we are not careful, we can quickly gloss over one of the letter's most basic intents. Paul's simple desire was to pat the Thessalonians on the back for the great work they had done and to encourage them to keep it up. This intent is at the heart of chapter 1 of 1 Thessalonians. As N. T. Wright notes, "the First Chapter of the letter is Paul's way of saying 'thank you' to God for the Thessalonians, and of encouraging them as well by telling them he is doing so" (93).

In this first chapter, Paul literally gushes with praise for the Thessalonians in light of their ". . . work of faith and labor of love and steadfastness of hope in our Lord Jesus Christ" (v. 3, NRSV) In the second half of the chapter, Paul highlights two commendable aspects of the Thessalonians' faith that are particularly worth noting. In vv. 6 and 7, Paul points out that the Thessalonians have become "imitators" of the example set by Paul and his companions and, thus, "imitators" of the Lord as well. The Greek term here is *mimetai*, from which we derive the term "mimic." As Beverly Roberts Gaventa points out, this is a use of the idea of imitation in the best possible terms. It wasn't that the Thessalonians were providing a counterfeit version of the gospel, i.e., an "imitation." Rather, they were perfectly modeling the Christian faith that had been set before them through Paul, Silas, and Timothy (Gaventa, 15-17).

Paul continues his pep talk in vv. 7-9 by making the Thessalonians aware that word has gotten out about their faithfulness. They had become an example to other congregations all over the area. According to Paul, before he and his colleagues could even tell others about the Thessalonians, folks they met were often telling them about the Thessalonians instead. In fact, one wonders if the reason Paul was so eager to send Timothy back to the Thessalonians was to discover if what they were hearing from these other believers in the area could possibly be true!

I am reminded of a remarkable lady in my home church that I knew while growing up who had the spiritual gift of letter writing. Every year on my birthday and at other significant occasions, I would receive a handwritten letter in the mail from her. These were not quick notes of "happy birthday" and a signature. No, in each letter she found time to affirm who I was and what I was becoming. Her comments always encouraged me to remain true to the principles I had set for my life. These were not merely birthday cards; they were significant words of encouragement that served to renew my resolve and refocus my priorities.

Paul's letter must have functioned in this same way for the fledgling church in Thessalonica. In the midst of intense persecution and questions as to whether this new faith was worth all the trouble, Paul's praise provided welcome words of encouragement at just the right time. This was their spiritual parent saying to them, "well done, good and faithful servants."

The Thessalonians as Encouragers of Paul and His Companions (1 Thess 3:6-10)

In a rather unique turn of events, a careful reading of 1 Thessalonians leads to the realization that the letter doesn't stop with Paul's attempts to encourage the Thessalonians. It also finds Paul rather poignantly stating that the Thessalonian believers have provided great encouragement to him and his companions too.

Our best guess is that Paul was in Corinth when he wrote to the Thessalonians. We know from the New Testament that Corinth was not an easy stop for Paul either. There too, as had been the case in Thessalonica and as would be the case in so many other places Paul would visit, his message was met with great opposition and danger. With the Thessalonian experience behind him and the Corinthian experience in front of him, it is easy to see how Paul could have been discouraged in the midst of such troubling and difficult occasions. To hear that the Thessalonians were doing well, that they were maturing in their faith, and that their resolve was strong was a tremendous boost to Paul's own sense of self-worth and the value of his mission.

One truly cannot underestimate how significant news of the success of the Thessalonian church was to Paul and his fellow missionaries. Among the most compelling signs of the value of this news to Paul is the word choice used in 1 Thessalonians 3:6 as he speaks of learning from Timothy the "good news" of the Thessalonians' continued faith. The Greek term Paul uses here that is translated as "good news" is the same from which we derive the term *gospel*. This is the only time in the entire New Testament that the term is used in a way unconnected to the "good news" of the saving work of Christ (Hobbs, 275). For Paul and his friends, receiving word that the Thessalonian believers continued in their commitment to the faith provided a tremendous boost.

Similarly, over the course of my ministry, I have received numerous letters from individuals and families thanking me for my help, guidance, presence, or leadership in a particular situation or event. Some of those letters have found their way to the center drawer of my office desk. When I have had a bad day, feel that I am not accomplishing anything, or simply want to throw up my hands, it is not uncommon for me to pull out one of the letters and reread it. Past successes have a way of renewing our energies and spirit in the midst of present adversities.

Timothy's report from Thessalonica had this same sort of effect. Yes, Paul wanted the Thessalonian believers to be encouraged by his words and prayers for them. He also wanted them to know that the fact that they were still plugging along, committed to Christ, and grounded in their faith had already served as a significant shot in the arm for him. No doubt about it, their faithfulness had brought significant encouragement to Paul.

Lessons from Thessalonians

At first glance, it may seem as though the central truth and lesson from this first session is a no-brainer. After all, who doesn't realize the significance and importance of encouragement?

It is true that there is no "rocket science" here. Yet, the fact of the matter is that many of the truly important aspects of life may be simple in their scope and yet profoundly ignored in our everyday activities of life. It doesn't take a lot of effort to pat someone on the back, drop a note in the mail, or simply call a friend to say that you are thinking about them. Still, how many of us take the time to do those things regularly and to realize that such simple acts are the ingredients of the kingdom of God? Making a real and meaningful difference in another human being's life can actually be as simple as a quick e-mail or taking a second to say "hang in there, what you are doing is really important." Yet, how often do we stumble past simple things in order to get to the important stuff of life that doesn't matter much in the end?

Encountering the words of encouragement from Paul to the Thessalonians and reading of the profound way their faithfulness had bolstered the apostle and his own ministry should serve as a strong wakeup call for all of us. Whose life have we failed to touch by ignoring the still, small voice that urges us to drop a card in the mail?

It is also likely that these passages from Thessalonians and this session have brought back memories of important words, actions, or letters from others that have served as timely instruments of encouragement in our own lives. Through these verses we have been reminded of the important role others have and can continue to play in our own sense of the value of our lives and how we choose to live them. These words call each of us to stop and join Paul in giving thanks to God for those who have taken the time to say "job well done" or provided a needed hug at the right moment.

1. What comes to mind when you think of 1 Thessalonians? Have you always associated 1 Thessalonians with encouragement, or is this an aspect of the letter that you have often overlooked?

_____

_____

_____

_____

_____

_____

2. What amazes you the most about the resilience and faithfulness of the early church at Thessalonica?

_____

_____

_____

_____

_____

3. Put yourself in Paul's shoes. Do you think you would have taken the time to write to your old friends in Thessalonica? Why or why not?

_____

_____

_____

_____

_____

_____

4. In your opinion, what is the most significant thing Paul writes to the Thessalonians in chapter 1?

_____

_____

_____

_____

_____

Live Caring for Others—Encouragement

5. Were you surprised to learn that Paul too needed to be encouraged? Why is it hard to believe that the great apostle may have wondered at times about the value of the work he was doing?

_____

_____

_____

_____

_____

6. How do you generally view small, simple acts of encouragement? Do you see them as truly significant ordo you often dismiss them as of little importance?

_____

_____

_____

_____

_____

7. When was the last occasion you took time to encourage someone else in a tangible way? What did you do for the person? Why was it important for you to do this?

_____

_____

_____

_____

_____

8. When was the last time someone encouraged you? What did they do to encourage you? How did it make you feel? How was it significant for your life?

_____

_____

_____

_____

_____

Live with Integrity—Behavior

1 Thessalonians 2:1-12; 4:1-8

Central Truth of the Session

As the old saying goes, "talk is cheap." Actions that back up our words, though, are something altogether different and ultimately much more powerful. The two sections of 1 Thessalonians considered in this session deal with issues of integrity, behavior, and, ultimately, holiness. The linchpin of both passages is the reality that commitment to God must manifest itself in the way we live our everyday lives. In the same vein, these texts encourage the reader to recognize that our actions rather than our words carry the most weight when it comes to societies' understanding of both us and our faith.

The Intersection of Thessalonians and Today

An interesting television commercial seizes my attention every time it is aired. There is no dialogue in the thirty-second spot, as only background music and scenes being played out on the screen are used to convey the message. The piece begins with one person doing something kind for another. Unbeknownst to the good Samaritan, a bystander happens to notice the act. The observer is so moved that he too does a good deed for someone, which again is observed by an outsider. This spectator is also led to help a stranger, and on and on the commercial moves as one good deed creates a domino effect for multiple and numerous good deeds.

Regardless of what the advertiser wanted to accomplish with this commercial beyond selling their product, the ad does a great job of getting at the heart of one of the basic tenets of the Christian faith. Whether we realize it or not, others are always attentive to what we choose to say and how we choose to act. The scary thing is that the judgment calls we make every day may quickly lead observers to make positive or negative decisions about the faith we claim.

The Thessalonian Context

While these two chapters of 1 Thessalonians may appear to have nothing in common with each other, behavior is obviously the important aspect for to Paul in both texts. Although separated by chapter 3, both chapters 2 and 4 revolve around issues related almost exclusively to this subject. In chapter 2, Paul seeks to put to rest any question of what motivated he and his two missionary companions to spend a great amount of time and risk a great deal in their visit to Thessalonica.

In chapter 4, Paul returns to the issue of behavior. This time, the focus is not on defending his own actions; rather, Paul turns his attention to the question of what it meant for the Thessalonians to live appropriately in regard to sexual behavior.

As we shall see, part of the reason Paul's words in chapter 4 were so important is because of the world within which the Thessalonians lived. Most scholars agree that the Thessalonian church was mostly, if not completely, composed of Gentiles (non-Jews). Coming from this background, their understanding of sexual ethics was likely far different from that of the Jewish society from which Christianity was emerging at the same time. The ideas of Judaism conveyed by Jesus regarding sexual purity would have likely been lost on the Thessalonians as a totally foreign approach. Therefore, the need for Paul to help the young believers craft an appropriate understanding of sexuality in light of their newfound faith would have been essential. While Paul likely spoke of these things with the Thessalonians during his short time in the city, a great deal of learning and maturing was still needed.

Unquestionable Motives (1 Thess 2:1-12)

Scholars are mixed when it comes to trying to piece together the background that led to the words of Paul in chapter 2. The majority sees these words as growing out of suspicions in Thessalonica concerning Paul and his companions' true motives for being there. It seems that these suspicions led to charges of mixed motives (v. 3), self-flattery (v. 4), and greed (v. 5). We don't know whether these accusations came to the surface during the short time that Paul and his friends were in town or after they left. But it is widely known that religious hucksters and spiritual charlatans were part of the landscape during the New Testament era and thus it would not have been abnormal for the three missionaries to be viewed skeptically.

In fact, in his commentary on 1 Thessalonians, noted Scottish biblical scholar William Barclay points out that the first Christian book of order called *The Didache*, which dates to about AD 100, already included a section dealing specifically with false teachers and how they were to be treated (189-90).

Several biblical scholars, on the other hand, do not believe that actual finger-pointing from Thessalonica led to these rather bold words of Paul. They suggest that it was quite common during that period for someone to establish their character by pointing out the things they opposed. From this perspective, Paul's statements about hidden agendas, self-importance, or greed were not directed at critics but were merely a way of establishing a clear picture of those characteristics to which he and his companions were utterly opposed (Gaventa, 25-26).

No matter which perspective you take, the heart of what Paul has to say in this section remains the same. When it came to his work, along with that of Silas and Timothy, their actions spoke for themselves and served as a solid witness of their impeccable motives among the Thessalonians.

After all, as Paul so astutely points out in the first two verses of the section, would they have undergone such persecution and difficulties if they were only in this business for fame or money?

Think about it for a moment. Paul and his companions had been mistreated in Philippi before coming to Thessalonica (2:1), and, as has already been established, they were also victimized while in Thessalonica and ultimately forced to leave after only a short stay because of the impending dangers. Does someone who is motivated only by deceit, money, or popularity willingly undergo such hardships?

The end of the section also finds Paul offering another example of why such accusations don't make sense in their regard. Verse 9 is a reference to how hard Paul and his companions worked while in Thessalonica so as not to be a financial burden to anyone there. Interestingly, it is not that Paul had difficulty with the idea of some type of payment for those serving the church (see 2 Thess 3:8-9). Instead, he simply chose not to receive anything for himself.

Paul points toward his labors as a way of dismissing the idea that he was only working among the Thessalonians for financial gain. The truth of the matter was that he didn't ask them for personal financial assistance even on those occasions when he felt justified to do so!

Rather than those of a religious huckster, Paul suggests that their actions among the Thessalonians were more in line with those of a wet-nurse caring for a beloved child (2:7) or a father teaching his children (2:11). In other words, like trusted members of a family who act out of love, care, and the well-being of others, this had been their disposition and attitude toward the Thessalonians.

One must back away from the words of Paul for a moment and admit that what the apostle has to say here is quite daring. It would have been ludicrous for him to attempt to say such things if there were no actions to back them up. Obviously, Paul's statements here were paralleled by similar actions. Otherwise, there is little likelihood that the Thessalonian believers would have preserved such claims. Instead, they would have dismissed the claims as unsubstantiated religious rhetoric.

Perhaps most daunting about this section of the letter is to risk asking whether twenty-first-century Christians could mount a similar defense against modern charges of mixed motives, self-aggrandizement, or greed by pointing toward our own actions.

A Call to Live Differently (1 Thess 4:1-8)

On the opposite end of the spectrum are Paul's words in chapter 4. Here the issue is not in Paul's defense of himself, but, sexual ethics. Nonetheless, our actions and behavior remain at the heart of the text. In terms of the situation surrounding chapter 4, we have already alluded to the fact that Gentile and Jewish ethics were two different animals. This is not to suggest in any way that all Gentiles in ancient Macedonia were perverse and without moral guidelines. But, at the same time, it should be noted that during the biblical era, sexual expression outside of marriage even as a part of pagan worship demonstrated a light regard for the sanctity of marriage. Such behavior was considered normal in Gentile Thessalonica.

It is also important to recognize that what would ultimately become a New Testament perspective on sexual ethics was at the time being shaped by Paul and his fellow New Testament writers out of their understanding of Jesus and Jewish thought on the subject. Paul's teachings, in all likelihood, meant covering new ground for the young Gentile converts in Thessalonica.

Basically, Paul focuses on three areas of sexual ethics in this section of chapter 4. First, he argues that sexual relations are to be constrained to a monogamous married relationship (4:3). Second, he suggests that for believers, the act of marriage should be seen as sacred rather than trivial and temporal (4:3-4). (One should be aware that there are numerous ways to translate the Greek term *skeuos*, which means "vessel" in v. 4. Some understand vessel here to mean the body, and others believe the proper translation is wife. Obviously, I am siding with the RSV here in choosing wife as the appropriate translation. Regardless, the idea of faithfulness within marriage is inherent to Paul's thoughts in vv. 3 and 4.)

Finally, Paul touches on the importance of considering the marriage of others to be sacred too. One should not covet a brother's wife or end one marriage simply to begin another with someone else with whom he or she is infatuated at the moment (4:6-7).

Paul also wanted the Thessalonians to recognize that these are not merely rules for the sake of rules. There is something uniquely spiritual about how we treat our own bodies and how we honor the bodies of others. In Pauline thought, the body was understood as God's temple. This is what Paul is eluding to in 4:8 when he says, "therefore whoever disregards this, disregards not man but God, who gives his Holy Spirit to you" (RSV). Just as the Hebrews recognized the Israelite temple as the place were God dwelled among his people, now Christians, as people of the new covenant, believed that God had taken up residence through his spirit in the new temple of our bodies. To say the Holy Spirit lives in us is to say our flesh and blood houses the very presence of God.

One way to interpret these verses is found in suggesting that our bodies as God's temple are to be treated with the same reverence, respect, and holiness with which the Hebrews treated the original temple. This line of thinking says that bodies no longer belong to us; they are God's instruments and thus must be treated and maintained in light of God's commands (Wright, 117-18).

Since this was a 180-degree change for the Thessalonians, Paul certainly had to exert a willingness to be redundant and patient when it came to this subject. Nonetheless, Paul expected that as followers of Christ, they would live up to the high calling of the gospel.

Similarly, we live in a period in which there is increasing openness and laxity when it comes to sexual expression and freedom. Marriage is not necessarily seen as being sacred, nor is sexuality generally understood as something that must be reserved for after marriage. Despite modern perspectives, the idea of the body as the temple of God remains an appropriate biblical perspective.

Lessons from Thessalonians

Both sections of 1 Thessalonians considered in this session contain the interesting Greek verb *peripateo*. The word is found in 2:12, where it is translated "to lead" in the NRSV, and it is also found in 4:1, where it is translated "to live" in the NRSV. *Peripateo* when literally translated means "to walk" and carries with it the idea of behavior. Paul is drawing a beautiful word picture here as he calls believers to live each day in line with God's commandments through putting one foot in front of the other in the practice of faith.

When we live in this way, it will be obvious to the world around us that we walk "to the beat of a different drum." We will stand out in our world and others will take notice. Despite how we may try to discredit the idea sometimes, our witness is almost completely tied to how we live. Only when our bodies truly become the temple of God will others encounter this One who wants to take up residency in their lives as well.

Before leaving this subject, one should also recognize that the Thessalonian predicament is just one aspect of the larger issue of seeing our bodies as being God's temple. You or I may do well with issues of sexual morality, but that doesn't necessarily mean we have mastered the art of reverencing our bodies as belonging to God and as being the dwelling place of God. Abusing our bodies through poor diet, lack of rest, substance abuse, or any other means is just as much a failure to appreciate the holiness of our bodies as any lewd sexual practice in which the Thessalonians might have involved themselves.

1. What role have the lives of others played in shaping how you have lived out your own life?

_____

_____

_____

_____

_____

_____

2. How have the actions of other believers shaped your faith in both positive and negative ways?

_____

_____

_____

_____

_____

_____

3. Can you recall a time when your own behavior as a Christian was watched by another and led to either a positive or negative response? Describe the experience.

_____

_____

_____

_____

_____

_____

4. Could you boast as confidently as Paul that your actions and motives in daily life are above reproach? Why or why not?

_____

_____

_____

_____

_____

_____

5. What role do you think sexual ethics play in the life and witness of the church today?

_____

_____

_____

_____

_____

_____

6. When it comes to properly addressing matters of sexuality, where does today's church do well and where does the church struggle?

_____

_____

_____

_____

_____

_____

7. Do you generally expand the scope of the idea of the body as the temple of God to include diet, exercise, rest, choice of words, etc.? If so, how? If not, why not?

_____

_____

_____

_____

_____

_____

8. In all honesty, do you think most believers recognize how much more important our behavior is than our words? Explain your anwer.

_____

_____

_____

_____

_____

Live Despite Hardships—Persecution

1 Thessalonians 3:1-5; 2 Thessalonians 1:1-12

Central Truth of the Session

In the life of faith, persecution should be understood as a given. Certainly hope and joy are also proper adjectives for a life lived in relationship with Jesus. But we must never dismiss the reality that living in step with God always means living out of step with the culture. This session will focus on Paul's complete honesty with the Thessalonians when it came to hardships and the question of suffering.

The Intersection of Thessalonians and Today

In a recent edition of *Time* magazine, the cover story asked the question, "Does God Want Christians to Be Rich?" This intriguing article investigated modern expressions within the church of the age-old theology connecting God and wealth. Known as the "prosperity gospel," the idea is that faithfulness to God will ultimately lead to wealth in terms of possessions and monetary gain. Within this framework, the equation is that if we seek spiritual riches, ultimately we will also reap abundant wealth in the here and now. (*Time*, 48-56)

Truth be told, there is nothing new or particularly modern about this way of thinking. In fact, biblical scholars trace a similar mode of thought all the way back to the Old Testament book of Deuteronomy. There a way of thinking about God emerged that suggested life plays out in a rather easy to understand and predictable way—if you obey God you will be blessed, but if you disobey God you will be cursed.

The later Old Testament writings disavowed this idea (think Job), and the words of Jesus certainly put things in a different light.

Yet, the idea that emerged with Deuteronomy and that continues to be perpetuated by spiritual health-and-wealth congregations today exists as an undercurrent in many believers' lives. Most of us may not say it quite as overtly as some of the folks interviewed for *Time*'s article, but in reality our thinking may not be extremely different. Despite what we might say, most of us still associate positive results in our lives with the blessings of God and negative events with God's disapproval. The words we encounter from Thessalonians in this session offer a significant corrective for such thinking. Paul's perspective is at once helpful and easy to affirm. At the same time, it is convicting and quite critical of much modern thought regarding God and well-being.

The Thessalonian Context

Paul and his team had formed a bond with the young believers in Thessalonica during their short sojourn there. It is obvious through a careful reading of these letters that there was much mutual admiration between the three missionaries and the young congregation that they had hastily left behind. In light of this love, it is easy to see how difficult it was for Paul and his companions to be separated from their friends with no way to contact them quickly and see how things were going. They worried and fretted over the toddler congregation until they couldn't stand it any longer. Ultimately, with the three now in Corinth, a representative (Timothy) was sent back to Thessalonica to check on the church in person.

The fears of the team were confirmed when Timothy returned to report that the Thessalonians were facing significant persecution and hardships. The good news was that the young believers were weathering the storm exceedingly well. Their resolve was strong and their commitment to their faith continued. Nonetheless, it also appears that Timothy returned to pass along to Paul and Silas the concern that questions had begun to arise in the minds of the Thessalonians regarding their persecution. We are not sure what these questions were, but modern scholars suspect one of two primary possibilities.

One thought is that there were those within the group who suggested that the persecution was a sign of God's displeasure with them. They had failed God in some way and because of their sins God was punishing them.

The other idea is that family members of the young Christians may have been begging them to come to their senses and to realize that if they gave up these silly beliefs in Jesus or at least curbed them a bit, then all of their suffering would likely cease. (Wright, 108-109)

Whatever the situation, it appears that the Thessalonians were being tempted to abandon ship. In light of this, Paul takes great pains in both 1 Thessalonians 3 and in 2 Thessalonians 1 to provide encouragement to this small beleaguered band and to help them put their sufferings in proper perspective.

Gospel Honesty (1 Thess 3:1-5)

In the face of the Thessalonians' questions about their suffering, Paul takes time in his letter to reiterate what he had obviously said while he was teaching and preaching in Thessalonica. The apostle makes his perspective clear in the second half of v. 3 and in v. 4 of this section: ". . . Indeed, you yourselves know that this is what we are destined for. In fact, when we were with you, we told you beforehand that we were to suffer persecution; so it turned out, as you know" (NRSV). From the way he phrases his comments, it appears that these words about the possibility of suffering were among Paul's initial statements to the believers, even as they were in the process of considering whether to cast their lot with Jesus or not.

What Paul wants to make clear is that such suffering should never be seen as a sign of God's displeasure. Quite the contrary, when we suffer for the faith, more times than not it is a sign that what we are doing and how we are living is in lock step with the commandments of God. After all, to live in regard to the call of the Spirit is generally to live in disregard for the perspectives of the world. So the suffering of the faithful is often a sign that believers are on the right path, not the wrong one.

Paul's blunt response to the Thessalonian predicament provides true gems worth considering by modern believers. First and foremost, this section finds Paul being brutally honest regarding the realities of following Jesus. The Scriptures never promise that the call of Christ will be easy or without incident. Rather, over and over again, we are encouraged to recognize that the gospel is always worth the cost despite the consequences of obedience.

If you have ever participated in a congregation that celebrates the various services of Holy Week, you likely have a sense of how uncomfortable most believers are with the idea of suffering and persecution. Generally speaking, congregations are quite crowded on Palm Sunday and Easter Sunday, as these two days focus on hope, possibility, and triumph. But things often change when it comes to worship opportunities in between these Sundays of celebration.

Maundy Thursday, Good Friday, and other Holy Week services usually draw much smaller crowds. Some might suggest this is simply because most Christians are not used to gathering for worship at these times. This may be true, but just as likely is the reality that while we look forward to celebrating the triumphal entry and the resurrection, we have little interest in being brought face to face with the passion. Most Christians do not relish being reminded that obedience means following in Christ's footsteps by carrying our own crosses and living sacrificially.

Something else worth noting about this section of Thessalonians is that it appears that the persecution the believers were enduring came from outside the community of faith. Jewish individuals angered by Paul, Silas, and Timothy's teaching as well as Gentiles perplexed and disturbed by this new movement seem to have been the source of the group's difficulties.

Today, much persecution of believers still comes from outside the community. However, it is also true that today we sometimes receive our greatest opposition from those inside the family of faith. Being a Christian does not guarantee that one is always going to be supportive of what others believe God is calling them to do. Instead, our attempts at obedience occasionally draw anger rather than affirmation from fellow believers. This response from those within the family of faith can be particularly difficult to handle.

Apocalyptic Hope (2 Thess 1:1-12)

In chapter 1 of Paul's second letter to the Thessalonians, the theme of 1 Thessalonians 3 is continued, yet a different tact is taken. Again, Paul commends and encourages the Thessalonians in light of their continued faithfulness despite the cost. Here, though, Paul moves to a focus on Christ's return in light of present difficulties.

Without a doubt, this can be a hard section of the Thessalonian correspondence to understand completely and fully. There is much to be debated in this section, particularly regarding God's punishment of those who are themselves punishing the Thessalonians (vv. 6-9). In light of these difficulties, the important thing is to stay focused on Paul's main purpose within these verses. The primary purpose here is not what will happen to the enemies of God's people, but what will happen to God's people who have remained faithful in light of extremely harsh circumstances (Gaventa, 106).

A common feature of Paul's writings was apocalyptic Jewish thought. This means he believed the return of Christ was imminent and that it would not be delayed for any great length of time. A part of this same theology also included the notion that the ill treatment and persecution of God's people would be a significant sign that the end was coming soon. Such a perspective offered hope and encouragement to those who found themselves in such tumultuous situations. It was a way of saying "hang in there; help is on the way."

This idea is at the heart of what Paul wants to communicate in these initial reflections of the second letter. In a sense, Paul is once again providing a pep talk to the Thessalonian church. He builds up their self-esteem through his praises (vv. 3-4), and then he paints a picture of future glory in which Christ will return to provide vindication to them and to pass judgment on those who have harmed and wronged them (vv. 5-10). He ends the motivational speech by reminding the church that they are always in his and his companions' prayers and thoughts (vv. 11-12).

For the Thessalonians, in the midst of their situation and circumstances, Paul's words must have provided a welcome thought. Their sufferings were not abating and their situation within the overall metropolitan community remained dangerous. To believe that Christ in all of his glory might break into their world at any moment and deliver them was a cherished idea. These were certainly believers who would have been quick to say, "Come, Lord Jesus!"

It is interesting to compare the situation of the Thessalonians with believers in North America today. We may enjoy having a spirited debate about end-times theology, but our fascination with the subject is quite different from the perspective of our spiritual ancestors in Thessalonica. For us, end-times conversations are more like trying to solve a mystery novel. It is about untangling the clues and solving the puzzle. It has little if anything to do with a longing to escape harsh and brutal conditions where our very lives have been put on the line because of our faith. In America today, end-time talk sells many books and may make for must-see TV. In first-century Thessalonica, however, talk of the return of Christ meant a glimmer of hope in what seems to have become a hopeless and dark existence where one's life hung in the balance.

We should never discount the fact that there do remain believers all over the world who understand the Thessalonian predicament at this point. Suffering, persecution, and execution because of one's faith are realities that are still present in our world. Believers who exist today within such circumstances truly appreciate and welcome the thoughts and hope of Christ's return as painted by Paul in the picture 2 Thessalonians 1 creates. Fortunately or unfortunately, depending on your perspective, this is a section of the text that most modern American believers with our wealth and comfortable lives have little ability to comprehend or appreciate.

Lessons from Thessalonians

Many lessons exist within the verses considered in this session. These lessons are of particular value to modern Christians in the United States. In these texts, we encounter a bruised and battered group of young believers brought face to face with the honest realities of their situation and, at the same time, with the hope of a better and brighter future day.

In the midst of it all, we should be reminded that true faith in today's world almost always equals true suffering. If that is not at least occasionally the case in our own situation, it is more than likely time for significant introspection as to whether our lives are truly being lived in step with God. It might also call us to question whether our congregation is truly taking steps to follow wherever Jesus leads.

Paul's honesty in these verses also calls us to be careful how we speak to seekers about faith. Certainly we should emphasize the wonders of hope, love, relationships, and forgiveness found in Christ. But at the same time, we must never forget to echo Dietrich Bonhoeffer, who said that when Christ calls us, "he bids us to come and die" (99).

Finally, 2 Thessalonians 1 provides us with an intriguing opportunity to reflect on how the idea of the second coming intersects believers at different times and in different geographical locations. Is there any chance that New Testament believers would understand what we in present-day America have done with the theology of the end of all things? Likewise, is there any hope for comfortable Christians in the United States ever to truly grasp what Paul is seeking to communicate to the Thessalonians and to other believers in similar situations with his words about Christ's return?

1. In what ways do believers today sometimes connect difficulties in life with obedience or disobedience to God? Are you prone to this tendency?

_____

_____

_____

_____

2. How can believers do a better job of being honest with seekers about the sacrifices and difficulties of faith?

_____

_____

_____

_____

3. How often and in what ways do you truly suffer for your faith?

_____

_____

_____

_____

4. In what ways have you experienced persecution from the inside rather than outside the church?

_____

_____

_____

_____

5. Is your congregation ever viewed as being out of step with the community? Or is the congregation generally looked at as exemplifying municipal morals? How is this a good thing or a bad thing?

_____

_____

_____

_____

_____

Live Despite Hardships—Persecution

6. How would you characterize the American fascination with the return of Christ?

_____

_____

_____

_____

_____

_____

7. How is this fascination different from the perspective and meaning offered in 2 Thessalonians 1?

_____

_____

_____

_____

_____

_____

8. How often do you think about or pray for Christians in other parts of the world who are enduring persecution?

_____

_____

_____

_____

_____

_____

9. What is our responsibility, if any, to pray for believers in other parts of the world who find themselves in dire situations? Do you think these Christians assume that believers in the West like you and I are praying for them?

_____

_____

_____

_____

_____

_____

Live the Faith—Evangelism

1 Thessalonians 2:9-12

Central Truth of the Session

When most people hear the term "evangelism," unpleasant images often come to mind. The term often leads to thoughts of knocking on the doors of strangers, asking uncomfortable questions, and being rejected by individuals who are not interested in listening. In recent years, numerous Christian leaders have encouraged believers to rethink how one most effectively shares his or her faith with others. Their argument has been that relationships rather than confrontational conversations provide the best platform for faith sharing. Current scholarship related to how Paul went about spreading the good news suggests that the ideas of these modern leaders may have significant roots in the ancient practices of the preeminent apostle of the church.

The Intersection of Thessalonians and Today

Several years ago Bill Hybels, senior pastor of Willow Creek Community Church in South Barrington, Illinois, wrote a book with the church's evangelism trainer Mark Mittelberg titled *Becoming a Contagious Christian.* The book became a bestseller in the Christian world and spawned several companion studies and resources bearing the same name. In the work, the two argue for a form of evangelism that couches the process of sharing one's faith within the context of existing and future relationships.

One of the ways they convey their idea is through one of Mittelberg's sayings that "you've got to barbeque first!" His point is that if you have already established a friendship with someone who respects and appreciates you, that person is likely to listen when you talk about your faith. From Mittelberg's perspective, a friend is much more apt to listen than someone who doesn't know you and has no previous experience with you. (97-99)

Calvin Miller expresses this same perspective through the statement, "I have never won anyone to Christ who didn't like me first" ("Relational Evangelism"). To be sure, we all know the profound difference between sharing our deepest feelings with a trusted friend as opposed to doing the same with someone we have just met.

Since most folks immediately associate negative experiences with the term "evangelism," they are likely to resist sharing their faith. *Relational evangelism*, which is the term used to describe the idea expressed by Hybels, Mittelberg, Miller, and others, seeks to place faith sharing within a much more relaxed setting. The hope is that as we become comfortable with this approach, we will be more likely to make our faith a natural part of conversations with others.

The Thessalonian Context

The book of Acts places Paul's primary method of evangelism within a rather predictable scenario. According to Acts, when Paul would enter a new city where he planned to minister and seek to plant a church, his first step was to make his way to the Jewish synagogue. On the Sabbath, Paul would take his turn before the assembly. As he did so, he would use the Hebrew Scriptures to turn the conversation toward the life and work of Jesus. As long as he was in the area and as long as he was allowed, Paul would continue to return to the local synagogue in order to preach, teach, and dialogue with anyone who would listen to him proclaim Jesus as the long-promised Messiah. Thus, Acts portrays the synagogue as Paul's main base of operation (Ehrman, 127).

While we see this scene play itself out on numerous occasions within Acts' description of Paul's missionary journeys, we also learn that Paul spent a great deal of time doing something else. In every place Paul visited, he also spent a major amount of time plying his trade as a tentmaker.

The apostle was a unique character when it came to his perspective on congregational support for those who served as traveling missionaries. Paul believed it was perfectly acceptable and appropriate for congregations to care for early missionaries through monetary gifts and other resources such as food and lodging. At the same time, Paul never chose this practice for himself. Instead, Paul always chose to work and pay his own way wherever he went in service to the Lord. The situation was no different in Thessalonica.

Both 1 Thessalonians 2:9 and 2 Thessalonians 3:8 make it clear that Paul, Timothy, and Silas labored at their chosen trade while in Thessalonica.

Recent scholarship, particularly through the work of Bart Ehrman, suggests that the daily labors in which Paul and his companions engaged may have also served another purpose. Beyond simply providing for the missionaries' financial stability, their occupation may have afforded them another natural forum within which to share the good news of Jesus. In fact, Ehrman suggests that this setting may have actually been a more important arena for evangelism than even the synagogue. (128-29)

Through the establishment and development of working relationships with local citizens, Paul and his team found fertile soul for telling the story of Jesus. To put a twist on Mittelberg's statement, in Paul's mind, working with someone may have been an important preamble to sharing the love of Christ with that same person.

Paul in the Thessalonian Synagogue (Acts 17:1-9)

As we explore the evangelism method employed by Paul while in Thessalonica, it is important for us to turn to Acts 17. This text provides us with our only supplemental information to 1 and 2 Thessalonians regarding Paul's work with the believers there. From Acts, we learn that Paul's stay in the area was a short one and that the Jewish and other municipal leaders worked in tandem with one another to have Paul and his team removed from the city.

From these verses in Acts, we also learn that Paul taught in the Thessalonian synagogue for three Sabbaths. Through this information, many have gathered that Paul was only in the area for three weeks before being forced to move to another community. Others are less specific and prefer to say only that Paul's stay was very brief. They argue that the fact that Paul appeared in the synagogue on three Sabbaths does not necessarily mean he was in the city for only three weeks.

What most seem to agree upon in light of these verses, though, is that Paul did indeed see the Thessalonian synagogue as the bedrock of his evangelistic efforts in the city. According to the text, Paul and his group may have used the home of Jason, an apparent local convert, as a location for worship and study (see Acts 17:5-9), but the synagogue seems to have been home base for Paul and his attempts to convey the good news of Jesus to the masses.

The Missionaries at Work (1 Thess 2:9-12)

When reading Paul, we sometimes encounter points where the apostle's retelling of his missionary work in Thessalonica differs from Luke's remembering of the events in Acts. At such points of variance, the general rule of thumb is to trust Paul's own recollection over Luke. After all, Paul's writings come directly from the source.

One case in point is the absence in Paul's letters of the time spent in the Thessalonian synagogue. Certainly one could say that this bit of information may simply not have been important in the grand scope of what Paul wanted to focus on in this short correspondence. Just because Paul didn't mention his time in the Thessalonian synagogue doesn't mean he didn't speak there, nor does it mean the work there was not significant. At the same time, it does stand to reason that the fact would have come up somewhere in the eight chapters that compose the two letters.

What is emphasized over and over again in these letters is the physical labor Paul and his companions did while in the area. At the outset, one must say that there definitely was an ulterior motive in the mention of their hard work. It appears that there were believers in Thessalonica who had allowed their belief in the nearness of the second coming (also called the *Parousia*) to cause them to quit working. These members of the congregation appear to have been merely sitting around while waiting for the end to come. In this passage, the hard work of Paul, Silas, and Timothy calls into question their laziness. This is a fascinating aspect of the letters and one that we will discuss at length in a later session.

Beyond this reason, Ehrman sees a further possibility. His sense is that the trio's work environment played a prominent role in the group's overall game plan for sharing their message with the people of Thessalonica (128-29).

What if Paul's workstation was also viewed as a holy place? What if the daily task of making tents or whatever other work the men did also provided the fertile ground for them to get to know the community and for the community to get to know them? What if people's admiration for Paul's craftsmanship and work ethic led to an openness to the missionaries' perspective on God's Son? Could it be that Paul taught as he worked, preached while he sweated, and counseled as he took work orders? If so, Paul was likely one of the original proponents of lifestyle evangelism as he viewed daily working relationships as fertile ground for gospel sharing.

Vocation and the Body as God's Temple

Think back to session 2, where we wrestled with Paul's understanding of the body as God's temple. The sense communicated was that our very being serves as the place where God's spirit resides. As N. T. Wrights says in *Simply Christian*, our bodies are one of the points at which heaven and earth overlap (128-29). This notion should lead us to recognize everything we do as being tinged with holiness and as activity ripe with God's presence.

Such thinking means that this same holiness is transferred onto our professional lives as well. This is an attitude that some within the church are trying to develop among believers today as they seek to encourage all of the people of God to recognize that our work is an extension of our faith. This is true for all of God's children, not exclusively for ministers. If our bodies truly are God's temple and if we embody the presence of God in the world wherever we are, then the Spirit desires to be just as present and alive in our work from 8 to 5 at the office as on Sundays at 11am. We fool ourselves when we believe that only a select few have been called to full-time Christian service. Instead, we should recognize that all those who claim the name Christian fall into this category.

Seeing our lives and our professions from this perspective should enable us to see our work as potential holy ground through which we might further the kingdom and share God's love with others.

Lessons from Thessalonians

Ehrman's novel way of thinking about Paul and his approach to his daily professional life provides us with a number of interesting ideas for discussion and reflection.

Among the most obvious is the way Paul appears to have leveraged relationships for the sake of sharing the gospel. The fact is that most believers are not comfortable with common forms of evangelism. At the same time, most all of us cherish the significant friendships in our lives and have no trouble sharing our deepest feelings and beliefs within the comfortable confines of these same relationships. While we may have been taught that religion and politics should always be off limits with our friends, we do need to affirm that both our comfort level and the receptiveness of the hearer to the gospel are much greater in these types of settings than they will ever be among strangers.

It is also interesting and worthwhile to think about the fact that Paul's relational evangelism seems to have arisen out of his professional life. One is certainly correct to suggest that we must be careful how we use our jobs for faith sharing. There are numerous methods and situations that are tactless and should be off limits. At the same time, we spend a great amount of our waking hours involved in our professional lives. Finding ways to allow our faith to be a larger part of our work as well as asking questions related to how we can use our professional expertise to advance the kingdom of God are crucial thoughts for the twenty-first-century church.

1. What do you think of when you hear the term "evangelism"?

_____

_____

_____

_____

_____

2. How do you distinguish between traditional evangelism and relational evangelism? Are you more comfortable with the former or the latter?

_____

_____

_____

_____

_____

_____

3. How do you feel about Ehrman's perspective on Paul's primary mode of evangelism in Thessalonica? Do you think this perspective has merit, or is it stretching the text too far?

_____

_____

_____

_____

_____

4. In what ways do you view your professional life as an extension of your faith?

_____

_____

_____

_____

_____

5. Beyond praying or an office Bible study, how can you use your professional skills to advance the kingdom of God?

_____

_____

_____

_____

_____

_____

6. What are the appropriate and inappropriate ways to merge your faith into your professional life?

_____

_____

_____

_____

_____

_____

7. How does seeing your body as God's temple change your perspective on daily affairs?

_____

_____

_____

_____

_____

Live Optimistically—Hope

1 Thessalonians 4:13-18

Central Truth of the Session

In this rather short passage from 1 Thessalonians 4, we find Paul addressing questions regarding those believers who have already died (note that some translations use the term "asleep" for death in this section of the text). Through the answers he provides, Paul's primary task is to infuse hope into what seems to be a hopeless situation. As he does so, Paul also helps us to recognize one of the hallmarks of faith that separates believers from nonbelievers—the ability to remain hopeful, even in the face of death.

The Intersection of Thessalonians and Today

Funeral etiquette and procedure has changed quite a bit over the last decade or two. It is not uncommon anymore for the visitation time and the funeral service to be held on one day rather than spread across a number of days. Likewise, services confined only to the graveside are becoming more popular as opposed to a service in a local church with a committal later at the cemetery. The days of black suits and somber dresses may be coming to an end as well. Today, you are just as likely to see guys in golf shirts and ladies in slacks when paying your respects to a family or attending the recently departed's funeral.

What hasn't changed over the years, though, are the traditional texts that are requested and read when people gather together to remember, reflect, and comfort one another. It is likely that almost any Christian funeral you attend these days will still include the 23rd Psalm, a recitation of the Lord's Prayer, or a reading of the story of Lazarus.

If you attend a graveside service, you are also likely to hear the words of 1 Thessalonians 4:13-18 read. All of these centuries later, Paul's words continue to serve as an amazing source of hope for the people of God. Here we find Paul assuring the believers in Thessalonica that the death of their brothers and sisters in the faith was not the end. Because of the death and resurrection of Christ and the promise of his return, there was reason to have hope. Paul provided assurance that their loved ones would live beyond the grave.

Obviously, the fact that these words remain so much a part of our own culture's attempts to wrestle with death speaks to the amazing power and sense of hope these same words continue to convey.

The Thessalonian Context

When Timothy returned to Paul and Silas after his checkup visit with the Thessalonians, he came armed with a number of questions from the young believers there. During their separation from one another, numerous events had happened in the lives of the Thessalonians that led to questions regarding how their new faith addressed the various mysteries of life. In session 3 we found Paul addressing questions related to the suffering that the Thessalonians were enduring. Again, we find Paul prepared to deal with a perplexing question for the young believers.

The issue was members in the Thessalonian church who had passed away in the interim between the first visit of Paul and his colleagues and Timothy's return trip. As has already been stated, Paul believed Christ's return was imminent. There is also much evidence to suggest that Paul believed he would still be alive as well when Christ returned. Interestingly, this belief can be seen in this section of 1 Thessalonians. Close attention to Paul's wording regarding those alive at the return in vv. 15 and 17 of chapter 4 finds him using the term "we," suggesting that he expects to be part of that group.

Since it is obvious that Paul had shared these thoughts with the Thessalonians, it seems they may have developed the idea that none of their membership would die before this event took place. When believers did begin to pass away, either due to the persecutions they were undergoing, illness, or simply old age, a major problem erupted. What about these now departed followers? In that they had died before Christ's return, had they missed out on the opportunity to experience the resurrected life? Was there any hope regarding these now deceased family members in the faith?

What is not certain is whether Paul's response to their questions provided a previously unknown perspective to the Thessalonians or if the words of Paul were simply a reiteration of things he had already attempted to convey during his visit that had been forgotten or somehow misconstrued (Smith, 723). Scholars offer various perspectives on this question and the text honestly provides little clue as to the answer.

Hope in Death (1 Thess 4:13-18)

One of the critical lines of Paul's entire response comes in the second sentence of the first verse of this section, ". . . you must not carry on over them (the deceased) like people who have nothing left to look forward to, as if the grave were the last word" (4:13, *The Message*). In the Thessalonians' confusion, they had begun to resemble the rest of society when it came to their response to death.

While there certainly were those within the Greek society of the time who held to a view of life after death, the majority of ancient Greeks understood death to be the end of life. There was no optimism or hope in the thought of life's end. As a result, the degree of grief, agony, and emotion connected with most funerals of the day was immense. Evidently, the notion among the Thessalonians that the now deceased among them had missed both the return of Christ and the chance for eternal life caused them to revert to this same type of grief that knew no comfort or hope.

It is important to realize what Paul is and is not saying in these verses. Paul was in no way suggesting that grief does not have a role in the Christian response to death. Instead, Paul's point was that grief should be accompanied by hope for believers who realize that death is never the final word.

Paul's response to the questions of the Thessalonians can be boiled down to two primary points. First, Paul reminds them that as people of faith, "we believe that Jesus died and rose again" (v. 14, NRSV). These words, which form a portion of one of the earliest Christian creeds, frame an aspect of Pauline theology that we find at other points in the New Testament writings such as 1 Corinthians 15 (Wright, 124). Paul's emphasis here is that belief in the resurrection of Jesus from the grave means also trusting that through Christ's power we will be able to know life beyond death. For Paul it is impossible to affirm Christ's resurrection without assuming the same reality for ourselves (see 1 Cor 15:12).

The second part of Paul's response to the Thessalonian question is the point that a proper theology of the Parousia (synonym for the second coming) includes understanding that those who are deceased will participate in the event. In vv. 14-17, Paul makes it clear that Christ's return is an event that will involve both those who are alive at that time and those who have already passed away. There are no special favors or bonuses for those who still happen to be on earth at that moment (Smith, 724).

Paul's Primary Intention

It is important to recognize that one can get quickly carried away with the poetic language and imagery Paul uses here. The apocalyptic phrases such as "archangel's call" or "sound of trumpets" as well as the scene of believers being reunited with the Lord in the air provides an amazing vision. Many have used Paul's rich vocabulary and picture of the future in this text to construct a literal version of how this portion of the return of Christ will transpire. To become bogged down in such activity is to miss the point of Paul's teaching. In these verses, Paul's effort isn't to explain how the second coming will unfold. Paul's intention here is merely to point out that the Parousia will not exempt those believers who have already died. They too will participate in this mind-boggling future day that will usher in the eternal reunion of God with God's people (Barclay, 203).

Embody Hope, 4:18

In light of the profound imagery found in this section of the text, one could easily gloss over the last verse of the passage with little attention or emphasis. This would mean making a significant mistake however, as these final words are quite significant and important. Notice how Paul ends this section in v. 18: "Therefore, comfort one another with these words" (RSV).

Paul had written these lines of the letter in order to address a significant concern among the Thessalonians. His ideas, however, were not a disconnected spiritual treatise on what happens to the deceased or what their role would be in the Parousia. No, these words remained couched in existing situations, and they would continue to be connected to real life as long as Christ continued to delay his return and as long as believers continued to pass away. In light of this, Paul says that they were to use these words in order to comfort one another.

As believers, we are to be people who embody hope. This does-n't mean we should ignore people's concerns, dismiss genuine grief, or act as though there is not a need to be sad. It does mean, though, that we should watch continually for appropriate ways to help others recognize that in Christ there is always hope in both the difficult circumstances of everyday life and in the midst of death itself. This is the word with which we should comfort one another, and it should serve as one of our primary witnesses to a world that has little reason for hope.

I have a good friend whose wife is struggling with cancer. Her condition is terminal, and her life expectancy appears to be a matter of months rather than years. As devout believers, they have agonized over how to express their perspective on this situation to others. In recent weeks, I have heard my friend say that when faced with questions about how they are doing, they have decided to say, "We are people of great faith in God, and our faith brings us great comfort in a time such as this." I like this response. It truly is Paul's response in this section of 1 Thessalonians. Our word to ourselves and to others must always be that as people of faith, we take great comfort in the hope we have in Christ even in the face of death itself.

Lessons from Thessalonians

It is unlikely that many of us can truly relate to how the Thessalonians felt in this particular instance. Here was a group that knew nothing of Christ or what was emerging as Judeo-Christian theology prior to the arrival of Paul, Silas, and Timothy. This reality, coupled with the fact that Paul and his companions were only among the Thessalonians for a short period of time, means they were trying to reorient their lives around a faith that was totally new and in many ways was barely explored or understood. There is no doubt that new questions arose in their minds every day. And, unlike in our world, there were literally no Scriptures, books, or people for them to turn to for help. The only other believers they likely knew were the three missionaries now a good distance away and inaccessible on a daily basis.

I paint this picture to suggest that this passage illustrates the type of patience Paul and his team had to exert with the Thessalonians. These were infants in the faith without a parent who was readily available. While we may not encounter many individuals today with no biblical basis at all, we do often find ourselves working with people whose faith and knowledge of the Scriptures is shallow and small. Like Paul with the Thessalonians, we must always accept people where they are instead of where we wish they were. In such instances, the key words are patience, understanding, grace, time, and love.

Ultimately, this session is a study in Christian hope. The theme here is hope in the face of death. If you've lived very long, you realize that there are countless other instances in life where Christian hope is also needed. This section of Thessalonians revolving around death serves as a springboard for other areas of life in which the reality of Christ's death and resurrection serve as an important symbol of hope and life in the midst of darkness and despair.

Verse 18, the final statement in this section, also serves as a significant reminder regarding our role in community life. Both in the community of faith and in the communities in which we reside, our Christian calling involves serving as people who embody comfort, peace, and possibility through the good news of the living Christ.

1. How difficult do you think it was to remain faithful to Christ as a member of the early church in Thessalonica? Beyond the persecution, how could one place faith in Christ with such little knowledge of his life or resources for continued study and learning?

_____

_____

_____

_____

_____

_____

2. Like the Thessalonians' questions about those who had died, what issue of faith or theology has raised questions for you over the years?

_____

_____

_____

_____

_____

_____

3. Do you see yourself as a hopeful person? Why or why not?

_____

_____

_____

_____

_____

_____

4. How should hope and optimism separate Christians from the rest of society? In what ways do we do a good job of providing this alternative perspective? In what ways do we do a poor job exhibiting hope?

_____

_____

_____

_____

_____

_____

5. Who are the people in your life that have embodied hope and optimism? How have these folks been significant to you over the years?

_____

_____

_____

_____

_____

_____

6. Beyond issues of death, what are the other aspects of our lives in which hope is desperately needed in our world today?

_____

_____

_____

_____

_____

_____

Live Optimistically—Hope

7. Do you think one of our primary responsibilities as believers today is to be people who embody hope? How is this sometimes done inappropriately? How can it be done in the most appropriate ways?

_____

_____

_____

_____

_____

_____

8. How does the church do today when it comes to the questions and missteps of new believers? Do we generally respond with the necessary amount of love and grace?

_____

_____

_____

_____

_____

_____

Live with Question Marks—Mystery

S e s s i o n *1 Thessalonians 5:1-11; 2 Thessalonians 2:1-12*

Central Truth of the Session

Part of our postmodern landscape includes a general attitude that life often does not make sense. Such a perspective leads our society to seek out people and places where important questions can be answered and life can find meaning. Naturally, the church is one of the primary places to which people often turn for such help. When this happens, we can find ourselves traveling on dangerous ground. Certainly the church should and must be a place that helps people make sense of their lives. At the same time, the church does not always have an answer for every question that is posed. Finding the ability to walk the tightrope between knowing when we can provide guidance and when we need to admit our limitations was difficult for Paul. It also remains a difficult balancing act for the church of today.

In truth, finding the courage to admit uncertainty can be a great gift to ourselves and to others. It is also a wonderful way to be reminded of God's sovereignty and our humanity.

The Intersection of Thessalonians and Today

Several years ago I participated in a funeral service for a lovely lady whose life had been cut short in her prime. I shared leadership of the service with another minister, and our approaches to the occasion were quite different. His desire was to help us try to make sense of the tragedy that was so heavy on all of our hearts. Through Scripture, theology, and illustrations, he attempted to explain what had happened in order to provide peace.

When I spoke, I made it clear that I had no idea why this tragedy had happened. I wasn't sure that it would ever be possible for anyone present in the sanctuary to solve the riddle posed by such a sad ending to life. I encouraged each person to do their best to continue to trust God through faith and to ask daily for God's assistance in living with the mystery. Certainly I wanted to affirm that God still loved us and would be with us in the days ahead. Yet it seemed to me that the only honest thing to do in that situation was to admit that we all had more questions than answers.

Our different perspectives that day mirror the hard place where we so often find ourselves as believers. We want to provide answers and solutions. We want our faith to help us sort out the puzzles. But, truth be told, such solutions are not always a possibility. Admitting that we don't have all the answers can seem to suggest insufficiencies within our faith. In reality, suggesting that life must be lived with mystery may be one of the most faithful and insightful responses of all.

The Thessalonian Context

As has already been stated elsewhere in this book, Paul firmly believed that Christ's return would take place before his own life ended on earth. This also appears to be a belief that the Thessalonians, through their time with Paul, had adopted for themselves. Unfortunately, as the days continued to pass along with business transpiring as usual, they likely became skeptical of Paul's teaching about the nearness of Christ's return. To make matters worse, as members of the congregation begin to die, the questions likely only intensified concerning the imminence of the Parousia.

Second Thessalonians 2 takes things a step further as it appears that the concerns regarding the delay of Christ's return had also led to a new teaching that apparently gained some popularity in the area. This idea, which we see most clearly fleshed out in 2 Thessalonians 2:1-2, was the thought that the return of Christ had actually already taken place and the believers in Thessalonica had missed out.

In both 1 Thessalonians 5 and 2 Thessalonians 2, Paul works hard both to address the concerns about the Parousia's delay and to dismiss the notion that the event had already occurred. In these passages, Paul moves back and forth between pointing out that little is known of how the return will unfold and trying to provide some idea of what to be watching for.

In fact, as was mentioned in the introduction of this book, Paul's oscillation has led to the belief that he may not have actually been the author of 2 Thessalonians. After all, how could the same person be emphatic about an event occurring like a "thief in the night" (1 Thess 5:2) in one letter and just as confident in listing things to watch for in another?

One approach to finding middle ground between these two seemingly polar opposite chapters is to do our best to understand the position in which Paul found himself. Much like you or me, Paul wanted to provide guidance and direction in the midst of the Thessalonians' questions regarding the second coming. At the same time, the apostle also wanted to make it clear that how the end will occur is a great mystery. Indeed, even Jesus claimed to be unaware of the day or hour of his return (Mark 13:32).

Because of this careful balancing act, Paul provides both direction and honesty about human restrictions when it comes to this future event. In 2 Thessalonians 2, he tries his best to offer a few signs to be attentive to, and in 1 Thessalonians 5, he assists the young believers in recognizing their limitations on this subject. Throughout, Paul appears to struggle as he tries to be helpful while at the same time truthful about how little one can know regarding the way the end will unfold.

A Thief in the Night (1 Thess 5:1-11)

As he begins this section of the letter, Paul insinuates in v. 2 that he is preparing to address a subject that he and the Thessalonian believers had previously covered. These are not new ideas that Paul feels compelled to share for the first time. Rather, the need has arisen to restate something with which they had wrestled before.

Although he may have been tempted to step out on a ledge and share his personal beliefs about how the end would unfold, Paul wisely chose to stay within the bounds of the few things that could be said about the subject.

First and foremost, Paul made it clear that no one knows the precise date of Christ's return (vv. 1-2). In fact, all that one can truly say is that like a thief in the night (v. 2), or as the sudden onset of labor pains for an expectant mother (v. 3), the return of Christ will come suddenly and unexpectedly. In light of this, the proper Christian attitude is to be patient, alert, and watchful. If this is our demeanor, we will not be caught off guard. Rather, we will be as prepared as humanly possible for this future day that will signal the end of the age.

Without a doubt, much can be extrapolated from the words of Paul within this text. If we are not careful, we can find ourselves on wild goose chases that have nothing to do with Pauline thought as found in these verses. Staying close to the text means being careful to emphasize those things that were important to Paul; namely our inability to know when the day of Christ's return would occur, coupled with a call to a daily attitude of alertness and preparation as we continue to watch and wait.

Signs (2 Thess 2:1-12)

2 Thessalonians 2 seems to be an about-face from Paul's feelings in 1 Thessalonians 5. There his point was that Christ will come at an unexpected time. Here, amid questions about the possibility that the end has already come and gone, Paul spends time discussing signs that could signal to those who are alert that the day of the return is close at hand.

The primary sign is the coming of the *lawless one* who is the ultimate personification of evil. Throughout history, there have been numerous individuals who have opposed the people of God and the progress of the church. This was true within Paul's day and has continued to be true over the centuries. In the lawless one of 2 Thessalonians 2, Paul seems to have in mind both present and future opponents of believers. More importantly, Paul wanted to point toward the day when a final opponent would appear whose presence would signal the beginning of the end of life on earth as we know it. Paul's perspective here is very much in keeping with Jewish thought of the period, which pointed toward a final day in which evil would be embodied in human form as the definitive adversary of God's work on earth (DeSilva, 65-67).

The term Paul uses for this figure is "the lawless one" and not the more popular term one may be tempted to substitute here—the "antichrist," which actually comes from the epistles of John. That term, as used in the Johanine epistles, refers to those who taught false doctrine. The term is not used in the epistles to denote a final and ultimate opponent of God as described by Paul in these verses from 2 Thessalonians.

This entire section is tricky and has baffled biblical scholars for centuries. Perhaps nothing in the section is harder to understand than Paul's phraseology in vv. 6 and 7 regarding "the restrainer" of the lawless one. Who was this restrainer? No one really knows, but perhaps the most popular explanation offered is that this term refers to the Roman Empire itself. Though riddled with faults of its own, the empire did promote peace and order throughout the ancient world. Perhaps the sense here is that at least for a time, the structure of the empire would aid in keeping such disruptive forces at bay. One day, however, a figure would arise whose power would be unable to be kept in check even by the great Roman Empire. Paul is saying only God would be able to overcome such an evil force (DeSilva, 66-67).

Despite Paul's more specific comments in this section, exactly how and when all of this will happen remains cloaked in rich imagery. Paul's emphasis here seems to be that while some things can be said about these future days, a great deal remains a mystery.

Lessons from Thessalonians

For some reason, many modern believers have developed the idea that being a strong Christian means having an answer to every question. Behind such a notion is the idea that unanswerable questions might possibly suggest an insufficient faith. Unfortunately, there are grave and sinister dangers present in this line of thought.

To force one's self into always providing an answer to any question is to give answers at times that could be wrong, misleading, and harmful. Without a doubt, it is great when believers are able to shed light and provide meaningful help in the midst of life's great uncertainties. But forcing an answer when there isn't one out of a desire to insinuate that our faith provides all the answers creates a situation where everyone looses.

In these passages, Paul could most likely have said much more than he did about the second coming. But at some point he would have probably left the realm of solid theology and moved into speculation. The wisdom of these two passages in turn is not only what Paul chooses to say, but also what he chooses to leave unsaid. Paul was comfortable with the mysteries of faith. He didn't mind admitting that he didn't have all of the answers. Apparently, he wanted the Thessalonians to feel comfortable with the question marks too. With this approach, Paul not only taught about the coming Parousia, but he also gave sound advice regarding the importance of admitting our personal human limitations.

Something else should be noted before concluding this session. In her commentary on Thessalonians, Beverly Roberts Gaventa points out that Paul demonstrates his ability to recognize the questions behind the questions. In other words, with his responses here,

Paul showed that he understood that the Thessalonians were not only asking about Christ's return. They were also questioning the validity of the gospel in which they had placed hope and the ability of God to overcome the evil that surrounded them. As Paul answered their end-times questions, he also responded to their indirect questions by making it clear that the gospel message was trustworthy and the Christ would indeed come again. He also left no doubt that in the end, God would reign supreme over every expression of evil, especially the "lawless one." (Gaventa, 75-76)

When people come to us with their own questions, we too would do well to listen carefully to what they ask in both direct and indirect ways. Questions about death can also be questions about hope. Conversations about finding a Sunday school community can, at the same time, be a means of saying I need a friend or I am lonely.

Part of being in community with others means doing our best to be good listeners. As we give others careful attention, we, like Paul, will hear clearly both what is being asked and alluded to in the same questions. Such listening will only heighten our ability to care for others in the most helpful of ways.

1. What strikes you about both what Paul said and didn't say in these passages from Thessalonians?

_____

_____

_____

_____

_____

_____

2. Why do you think believers today continue to be so intrigued by the second coming?

_____

_____

_____

_____

_____

_____

3. Why do you feel it is so difficult for Christians to admit that they don't have all of the answers?

_____

_____

_____

_____

_____

_____

4. In your experience, what are the areas of life in which believers are most prone to go too far in their attempt to provide an answer or perspective?

_____

_____

_____

_____

_____

_____

5. Do you recall a situation in which someone's inability to admit they didn't have an answer caused more harm than good? If so, describe the situation.

_____

_____

_____

_____

_____

_____

6. Why is the reality of unanswerable questions and mystery a positive rather than negative when it comes to our faith lives?

_____

_____

_____

_____

7. If you had to communicate Paul's perspective on the second coming in Thessalonians in one or two sentences, what would you say?

_____

_____

_____

_____

_____

_____

8. How well do you think most Christians do when it comes to listening for both the verbal and nonverbal questions of others?

_____

_____

_____

_____

_____

_____

Live Ready—Alertness

Session   *1 Thessalonians 5:1-11*

Central Truth of the Session

In spite of modern Christianity's obsessions with dissecting the second coming of Christ in order to understand exactly how and when Jesus will return, the New Testament sets these future events within a much broader context. Implicit within the New Testament's teachings about the end times is the call for Christians to live with a sense of urgency. One day Christ will indeed return. In light of this reality, our lives should be shaped by a sense of awareness, alertness, and attentiveness to the coming end of the age.

The Intersection of Thessalonians and Today

As I write this chapter, my wife and I are anticipating the birth of our second child, now only a few months away. Having been through this experience with our daughter four and a half years ago, I know that as the day grows closer, we will begin to live with a heightened sense of expectation.

In a couple of months we will pack a suitcase for the hospital and begin sleeping with one eye open. As we go to work or spend time with friends, we will be aware that life could be interrupted at any moment by the arrival of our child. The realization that the due date is right around the corner will lead us to live every day with a new sense of readiness, alertness, and urgency.

This is the same prescription Paul suggested to the Thessalonians. Even though this is the passage considered in the previous session, this same text does a terrific job of focusing our attention on spiritual readiness.

As with my wife and I in anticipation of the birth of our son, when we are focused on an important upcoming event, the manner in which we approach the future is greatly altered. Some tasks suddenly become imperative and other things are no longer as significant as they once were. Such refocusing is a normal aspect of living ready and alert.

Paul wanted the Thessalonians to live with the tension of the return of Christ as an ever-present reality. His expectation was that the nearness of this event would lead the Thessalonians to shape their lives accordingly. As believers who continue to await the Lord's return, the mandate of the New Testament also calls us to approach each day with an attitude of readiness and alertness due to the coming of Christ.

The Thessalonian Context

If there is any passage with which we should quickly resonate in the Thessalonian correspondence, it is this text. After all, the same dangerous attitude that tempted the Thessalonians remains a temptation today in regard to how we view the second coming of Christ.

In all likelihood, while Paul was in Thessalonica, he communicated to the believers his sincere conviction that Christ would return during his lifetime. Yet, as the days and months went by and the promised event failed to materialize, the believers began to question the centrality and reliability of the promised Parousia as a part of their outlook and theology.

As mentioned in session 6, some in Thessalonica were teaching that the Parousia had already occurred and, consequently, the Thessalonian believers had just plain missed it (see 2 Thess 2). Apparently, some of the Thessalonian Christians were influenced by this idea. It may, however, be more realistic to assume that an even larger number had simply waned in their anticipation of the event as time progressed with no sign of the end in sight.

This attitude may be what Paul refers to in v. 3 of this text as he mentions people speaking of "peace and security." The idea of "Roman peace" or *pax Romana* was alive and well during this period in Thessalonica. The notion that one of the greatest benefits of the empire was the peace and security it offered to its citizens was seen as a crowning achievement of Roman rule. The phrase *pax Romana* was found on coins and celebrated at pagan altars. It was an empire-wide motto of sorts. Life was good and peace reigned. How could the Thessalonian believers honestly say that the world was in need of God's wrath or deliverance from evil? (DeSilva, 48)

So on one hand, the Thessalonian believers had the words of Paul ringing in their ears insinuating that the world was spiraling out of control and coming to an end. On the other hand, the Thessalonians were also being influenced by the delay of this event and the words of the empire that said all was good as peace, security, and harmony reigned.

We live with this same tension today. Scripture continues to call us to be awake, alert, and attentive as Christ could come at any moment. Yet, like the Thessalonians, we join centuries of believers who waited for this event throughout their lives. We also live in one of the wealthiest societies of all time that tempts us to see life as rich and abundant. What can be so bad about life that makes us need God's intervention or judgment?

People of the Day (1 Thess 5:1-11)

These eleven verses can be read in only a matter of minutes. Despite its brevity, the text overflows with Jewish apocalyptic imagery that calls for a posture of alertness while awaiting the coming day of the Lord. Through five different phrases, Paul repeats the importance of vigilance and watchfulness.

A thief in the night. In v. 2, Paul compares Christ's return to the unexpected presence of a bandit or robber. Sure, one might lock the doors, install a security system, or make certain that the motion lights are working, but, nonetheless, the presence of an intruder will make one's heart skip a beat. No matter how much we prepare, this remains an experience that we never seriously expect to happen.

Labor pains. The imagery in v. 3 is similar to the illustration of the intruder in v. 2. Again, the scene is one in which the elements of preparation and surprise are mixed together and become strange bedfellows. Yes, you can and should prepare, but when labor pains begin, no amount of preparation will have totally readied you for the occasion.

Day and night. Verses 4 through 8 offer a comparison of those who live by the light (daytime) as opposed to those who wander around in the darkness (nighttime). Once more, these are familiar apocalyptic terms and should be familiar to anyone who is a student of the New Testament. The Gospels depict Jesus as the light of the world (John 1:9). As his followers, we are children of the light (Matt 5:14-16). In other words, we have a guide who provides direction.

Live Ready—Alertness

We do not have to stumble around as does one who lives in the dark.

Soberness and Drunkenness. Also sprinkled throughout vv. 4-8 is the depiction of believers as sober or alert and nonbelievers as drunkards. Building on all the other phrases and descriptions, we again see Paul wanting to insinuate that Christians should "live" ready. Rather than being completely disoriented as someone who has become inebriated, followers of Jesus should be awake to what is happening in the world and to the implications of these same events for their faith lives and for the coming of the kingdom of God.

Being Asleep and Being Awake. Beginning in v. 6 and found throughout the latter half of the selected text, Paul also calls the reader to choose a posture of spiritual wakefulness over being asleep. Rather than resembling the disciples in the Garden of Gethsemane, we are called to maintain the vigilance and watchfulness associated with wide eyes, not the slouched shoulders of peaceful slumber.

If you carefully think through the various reasons why Christians should live prepared for the coming return of Christ, you discover something interesting: the overarching theme is readiness. At the same time, particularly in the use of such analogies as "thief in the night" and "labor pains," there is the realization that one can never be totally equipped for the Parousia. No matter what one does, there is always going to be an element of surprise involved, just as is the case with an intruder in your home or the onset of labor pains.

Certainly we don't need to overanalyze Paul's chosen analogies here. We also don't desire to detract from the centrality of preparedness for these verses either. Nonetheless, there is a significant gospel truth in recognizing that humanly speaking, not matter how well we dot our "i's" or cross our "t's," surprise will accompany Christ's return, even for the most faithful of believers.

Lessons from Thessalonians

This text abounds in practical lessons for modern believers who find the New Testament descriptions of Christ's return intriguing yet difficult to apply to everyday faith practice. First and foremost is the call to live attentively and alert to the realization that Christ's return could happen at any time. We must be careful with this directive, though, as this command can easily consume our energies and leave us so "heavenly-focused that we are of no earthly good." The need here is not to become paranoid but simply to live cognizant of the fact that we are never promised a life that will continue indefinitely.

In light of the relative prosperity of many modern Americans, it is also important that we help assist others in being awake to the fact that this world is passing away and that it will eventually give way to a better world. As with the *pax Romana* of the Thessalonian world, we have to work extra hard today in order to help our society understand that God will one day judge the world. In spite of how good we think our lives might be, faith in Christ is the only way to prepare adequately for that coming day.

Beyond the association of Christ's return with the ending of life as we know it, there remains another way that these words are practical. While this text has at its heart the second coming, it can also serve as a reminder that Christ is present in our world each and every day. Through the Holy Spirit, Christ wants to speak, teach, and call us to join in the kingdom's work. If we are not ready and alert to this reality, we may fail to recognize the Spirit's presence and heed the Spirit's call.

Interestingly, this theme is at the heart of the first Sunday of Advent in preparation for Christmas. The first Sunday of Advent is called the Sunday of expectation or hope. As the day calls us to focus on the hope found in Christ's return, it also calls us to look with hopefulness toward Christ's presence in our daily lives. This is a particularly significant word for the holiday season. In the midst of all of our Christmas business, it is easy to become so focused on the parties, gifts, and other items of the season that we fail to make time for a recognition of Christ in our lives. Before we know it, Christmas has come and gone and we have totally missed the opportunity to encounter the Lord.

Have you ever been in an airport, the mall, or simply driving down the road when you passed an old friend you hadn't expected to see? When this happens, it usually takes a while for us to realize who we have encountered. Because we were not expecting to see the person, we might easily walk right past them without recognizing them. The same is true in our lives of faith. We must live expectant of an encounter with Christ each and every day. If we are alert, we are much more likely to recognize and be open to Christ in the midst our everyday affairs.

Christ may not return for years to come, and the end of our lives on earth through death may yet be years away. However, we

can be certain that Christ through the Holy Spirit will continue to be at work in our lives in special ways in the days, weeks, and months ahead. If we are to make ourselves available to these future encounters, we must live open and alert.

How? There are many ways one could answer this question. Among the most valuable practices is regular involvement in a local community of faith for worship and Bible study. One should also make space for practicing spiritual disciplines like prayer, Scripture reading, journaling, silence, and fasting. All of these help us reorient our thinking and our lives toward the things of God and the kingdom of God. When we are pointed in that direction, we will be much more alert to the movement and presence of God in our lives.

1. As you read these verses from 1 Thessalonians 5, which phrase or phrases stand out in your mind as most informative of the need for vigilance while awaiting the return of Christ?

_____

_____

_____

_____

_____

_____

2. According to this session, what role did the pax Romana play in the Thessalonian society and people's inability to appreciate the call to be ready for Christ's coming? How does our own modern prosperity prevent many people from sensing the urgency that should be associated with preparing for Christ's return?

_____

_____

_____

_____

_____

_____

3. How would you evaluate modern Christendom's response to the call to prepare for Christ's coming?

_____
_____
_____
_____
_____
_____

4. In what ways does Christ, through the Holy Spirit, work in our lives in unexpected ways every day?

_____
_____
_____
_____
_____
_____

5. Do you remember a time in your life when you were unprepared for an event? How does that memory influence your desire to be ready for Christ's presence, however and whenever it may come?

_____
_____
_____
_____
_____
_____

6. What role can worship, Bible study, and the spiritual disciplines play in our preparation for Christ's presence?

_____
_____
_____
_____
_____
_____

7. In what ways do you generally connect worship, study, and the spiritual disciplines with spiritual readiness?

_____

_____

_____

_____

_____

_____

8. Do you agree or disagree with the assertion in this session that it is impossible to prepare ourselves totally for the coming of Christ? Explain your answer.

_____

_____

_____

_____

_____

_____

Live Skeptically—Investigation

1 Thessalonians 5:19-22

Central Truth of the Session

Believers often approach Christian ideas and theological thoughts with a degree of naivety. Rather than thoroughly considering what others say or taking the time to wrestle with their perspective, we often blindly accept what others tell us. Sometimes this acceptance is a result of spiritual laziness, as we would rather assume someone knows what he or she is talking about than take the time to do our homework. At other times, our respect for and trust in the speaker simply overrides the voice in the back of our minds that questions what we hear. For instance, if someone we admired was leading a bible study and quoted one of the gospels as saying that "God helps those who help themselves," we may not think twice. Unfortunately, our blanket of belief would mean never realizing this quote is actually from Benjamin Franklin rather that the New Testament.

Nonetheless, in the midst of myriad ideas and perspectives offered under the Christian banner today, it is imperative that we are diligent when it comes to testing and considering the validity of competing voices. As Paul said to the Thessalonians in these verses, a proper faith is one that approaches every new idea with an appropriate amount of skepticism and investigation. This has, and always will be, a Christian's right and duty.

The Intersection of Thessalonians and Today

A visit to the religion section of any large bookstore can provide a fascinating perspective on the wide variety of traditions alive and well within twenty-first-century Western Christendom. Not only can you quickly survey numerous approaches, but you can also find various ideas and viewpoints offered by equally devout believers on almost any topic or issue you choose.

It is clear that all of these competing voices require Christians to do their homework. It is impossible to accept each view proposed as valid and legitimate despite the credentials of the writer. If this were our attitude, we would quickly find ourselves having to accept one side of the coin on a particular issue today and the opposite side of the same coin tomorrow.

For all of its richness, Christian pluralism necessitates Christian responsibility on the behalf of every believer. This was true in the world of the Thessalonians and it remains true in our world today. As we shall see, the point is not Christian obstinance. Rather, it is the desire to recognize that as a follower of Christ, we are allowed to make personal decisions about what we will choose to include and exclude from our faith foundation.

The Thessalonian Context

Throughout the biblical world, competing ideas related both to proper theology and faith practice were quite common. In fact, if you read the New Testament closely, you will find the various writers working hard to dispel all kinds of wrong thinking and poor teaching.

One example is Gnosticism, which is combated throughout the New Testament. Gnosticism was a heretical movement that sought to boil faith down to a secret form of knowledge that only a select group could possess. Believe it or not, vestiges of Gnosticism remain alive and well in our world today.

Another example of early believers attempting to dispel heresy can be found at the center of 1 and 2 John. In these letters, the issue is the idea that Jesus was God, but, not a normal human being like you and me. This claim was dividing believers and causing all kinds of dissension. (See specifically 1 John 4:2 and 2 John 7.)

Thessalonica was no different. We have no way of knowing how large of an issue bad theology was in Thessalonica. But we do know that it was an issue that led to Paul's warnings and guidance in 1 Thessalonians 5. We also feel confident that it was a problem at least in terms of ideas being disseminated regarding questions about Christ's return.

As has been covered in other sessions, the first four verses of 2 Thessalonians 2 find Paul dismissing the idea that Christ's return had already taken place and reasserting that the Parousia remained a future event. This notion that Christ's return had already passed obviously found at least a significant minority of adherents within the young church. The question of where this teaching came from is one that we cannot answer. It could have been the product of members of the congregation and their own logic or poor understanding of Paul's teaching. It also could have come from other traveling teachers, like Paul, who had visited the new believers in Thessalonica and shared their own understanding of the faith. Regardless, the ideas were present and were having a negative effect on the well-being of the believers there.

Paul's Ethical Laundry List (1 Thess 5:19-22)

The four verses that are the focus of this session conclude a larger section of 1 Thessalonians 5 that begins with v. 12 and extends through v. 22. These verses make up a type of behavioral guide for the Thessalonians in terms of how Paul felt they should relate to and treat one another. Using Tom Wright's reflections, one could break the larger passage down into three sections with vv. 12 and 13 focused on respect for church leadership, vv. 14 and 15 devoted to the importance of caring for fellow members of the community, and vv. 16-22 serving as a final checklist for the young church's interrelationships (132).

Verses 19-22 fall within this final section and may at first glance appear to be verses that have little to do with one another. In fact, if one rushes through this section too quickly and sees it as merely insignificant concluding remarks, it would be easy to miss the value of these words altogether.

In his translation of the Scriptures called *The Message*, Eugene Peterson does a great job of conveying both the connectedness of these four verses and their overall significance. Here is how he renders vv. 19-22: "Don't suppress the Spirit, and don't stifle those who have a word from the Master. On the other hand, don't be gullible. Check out everything, and keep only what's good. Throw out anything tainted with evil."

Paul's command in v. 19 not to "suppress the Spirit" is connected to the words in v. 20 regarding "stifling those who have a word from the Master." As William Barclay points out, some translations use a version of the term *prophesy* in v. 20, but what is being described here are the actions of someone who led at Thessalonica as would a preacher or teacher in a modern local church. The point Paul is making is that the act of ignoring what a church leader has to say is a way of preventing the Holy Spirit from speaking to us and teaching us. (207)

Due to questionable teaching or preaching, such as the belief that the Parousia had already taken place, some within the Thessalonian church apparently had begun simply to tune out those who proclaimed God's word. Again, what Paul sought to remind them was that when they behaved in this way, they were preventing the Holy Spirit from having the opportunity to speak to and guide them. This concern leads Paul to argue for a happy medium in vv. 21 and 22.

Wisely, Paul did not suggest a posture of gullibility that would force the Thessalonian believers simply to accept any teaching or preaching that came their way hook, line, and sinker. At the same time, Paul didn't want the Thessalonians to close their eyes and ears as a result of previous bad experiences either. Instead, Paul argued for a stance in which everything was tested. When things were tested and thoroughly considered, the good could be kept and acted upon and the bad could be ignored or disregarded.

It should also be noted that Paul's instructions here are set within the context of community life. In other words, the testing that Paul advocates should take place within the fellowship of others. Rather than picking and choosing what we like and don't like as individuals, we should work at gauging good theology and bad theology with others. It is as we pray, read the Scriptures, and listen for God together that we are most apt to be able to discern the voice of God from the babble of human beings (Gaventa, 84-85).

Paul's tightrope walking here is done with skill and precision. Here we see the apostle at his best as he is careful not to advise *carte blanch* acceptance of what anyone says just because they claim their words are from God. At the same time, Paul strongly advocates openness to what others have to say despite the reality that past experiences might urge us to be suspicious. In the midst of it all, Paul recognizes and counsels that reflecting on ideas should be done within the context of Christian community where others can help us know that which should be held on to and that which should be rejected.

Lessons from Thessalonians

These words from Paul deserve our utmost attention. Navigating the modern Christian matrix is definitely not easy, and this reality is never truer than when the subject turns to the issue of recognizing both helpful and harmful teaching.

Paul's wisdom in this passage recognizes that Christians can easily fall into one of two camps that are both equally bad and dangerous. Some believers are completely open-minded to any idea or theological statement as long as it is cloaked in the appropriate amount of "God language" and the right spiritual terms are used. Other believers, jaded by past experiences or due to a pessimistic attitude, dismiss almost anything anyone says in the name of Christ. Again, both outlooks can be harmful.

If we fall into the category of those who are prone to accept quickly what others say, Paul waves a yellow flag of caution in our direction and calls us to tread carefully. We must be sure to process what we have heard, meditate on how it fits into our understanding of the Scriptures, and be certain that the ideas are in line with the teachings of the church.

If we are more likely to approach Christian ideas and theology with skepticism, Paul waves the same yellow flag in our direction and calls us to walk cautiously as well. We must appreciate the fact that God does continue to speak through his children and that there is plenty of sound theology and valuable Christian thought in the world today. To ignore teaching or preaching is to stick our fingers in our ears and hold back the Spirit of God. We must be open, keeping that which is good and throwing out that which is bad.

It should also be said that sometimes these guidelines from Paul can apply to our feelings toward a single individual. In other words, when we have had a bad experience with a teacher, preacher, or some other type of church leader, the past encounter can prevent us from being receptive to that person in the future. As a result, our attitude may keep us from a significant encounter or helpful and valuable word. A better approach is to be open to the person. This allows us to judge the person's words rather than being consumed with judging their lives. This perspective may very well lead to a valuable and unexpected experience.

Guides in the Search for Truth

This session also calls us to take a moment to consider the primary resources that can be helpful as we seek to distinguish between proper and improper Christian ideas. First and foremost, the Bible serves as our primary source in such work. We must compare what we hear with what we find in the Scriptures. Likewise, as we read the Bible, we must interpret each text through the life, work, and teachings of Jesus. After all, if Jesus was God in human form, then Jesus provides us with the best key for exploring all the Scriptures.

Another invaluable resource is prayer. Finding the space to sit quietly and listen for the voice of God is important to the process of discerning the truth. Unless we make the effort to stop and listen, it can be difficult for us to hear God's perspective.

Christian tradition provides important direction and insights too. Certainly God is not incapable of leading his people down new paths. But the centuries of Christian thought and action generally provide good grounding in how the people of God have felt about and responded to numerous situations down through the ages. Most of the time, these collective voices shed significant light upon our quest for sound understanding of the faith.

Finally, time spent in community with others is imperative. It is true that sometimes following Christ means breaking with the crowd and stepping out on faith alone. More times than not, though, weighing the claims and assertions of others in order to separate the "wheat from the chaff" is best done in conversation with others. The wisdom of others is always a necessary and essential aspect of the Christian journey. The suggestions of Paul in 1 Thessalonians 5 appear to have assumed that the work of distinguishing good teaching from bad would take place in the company of others. This underlying assumption should also be at play in our own efforts to seek truth.

1. In what ways do you regularly exercise the right to test the teachings of other believers? If you don't test others' words, why not?

_____

_____

_____

_____

_____

_____

2. Are you someone who is usually wide open and perhaps naïve when it comes to new ideas, or do you generally approach fresh theological thoughts with pessimism? Elaborate on your answer.

_____

_____

_____

_____

_____

_____

3. How have previous experiences shaped your particular approach to new ideas? Explain your answer.

_____

_____

_____

_____

_____

_____

4. Are you comfortable with seeing skepticism as a healthy Christian disposition, or does this seem like an oxymoron to you?

_____

_____

_____

_____

_____

_____

5. What role do Scripture, prayer, and tradition play in your attempts to judge new ideas as appropriate or inappropriate?

_____

_____

_____

_____

_____

_____

6. In your opinion, is our culture's haste to accept new ideas more a result of spiritual laziness or of great respect for those who lead us? Why do you feel this way?

_____

_____

_____

_____

_____

_____

7. Why is the notion of healthy Christian skepticism so important for our particular day and time?

_____

_____

_____

_____

_____

_____

8. Describe an experience in which a fellow believer's past statements kept you from being able to listen to or learn from them in the present?

_____

_____

_____

_____

_____

_____

Live Actively—Work
2 Thessalonians 3:6-13

Central Truth of the Session

It has often been said that when it comes to the church, "twenty percent of the people do eighty percent of the work." Obviously there is a certain degree of exaggeration in this statement. Nevertheless, there is great truth in the notion that many people approach the church with an attitude of receiving rather than giving. This same outlook was alive and well among a group of believers in Thessalonica who had stopped working. Like some modern believers, these Thessalonian Christians were living off the hard work of others. By looking at these elements of the early church in Thessalonica, this session will focus on the need for every believer to recognize the importance and necessity of hard work by every member of the body of Christ.

The Intersection of Thessalonians and Today

Buffet Christianity is a term used by some to describe a modern trend among believers in relation to their involvement in local congregations. Rather than choosing a church to be part of and immersing themselves in the life and work of that particular congregation, an increasing number of churchgoers are choosing to get involved in the various ministries of multiple congregations.

For example, instead of simply becoming a member of a church and participating in its ministries, I may choose a more varied approach. I may attend the worship service at one church, the Wednesday night study at another, send my children to programs at a third church, and participate in the fitness program at yet a fourth community of faith.

People with this attitude seek to find congregations that excel in each of the various facets of church life in which they are interested. Then they simply involve themselves with each of these different congregations. Adherents of buffet Christianity will likely never join any of the congregations in which they choose to participate. At the same time, they can also develop a dangerous perspective that is only concerned with what these congregations have to offer them. These believers rarely ask what congregations should expect from them.

This session's text from 2 Thessalonians is interesting in that it focuses on believers within the church who were not working and were thus living off the generosity and gifts of fellow church members. At first we may read this text and focus on what these words say about hard work in general. Just as important, though, is this passage's focus on the responsibilities of every believer within the life of his or her congregation. This dimension of the text can lead to focusing on those who refuse to do their part within the life of the local church. These "congregational freeloaders" may serve as a prime example of the Thessalonian disease that continues to manifest itself in our own day and time.

The Thessalonian Context

From the outset, it is important to focus upon Paul's expectation for the Thessalonians to live in community and harmony with one another. It doesn't appear that the Thessalonians operated like the Jerusalem church, where members gave property and other financial resources to the community for the benefit of all. But it does appear that Paul led the Thessalonians to refer to one another as family and to relate to one another in the way of a typical Mediterranean family of the day. Employing such a framework meant that when one family member was in need or unable to care for themselves, other members of the family would step in and see that those concerns, whatever they might be, were dealt with and alleviated.

What was happening among the Thessalonians was a situation in which some members of the congregation were taking advantage of the ministry and kindness of others. Some in the community were choosing not to work. They were idly squandering their days, apparently expending most of their energy attempting to make the business of others their own. These "busybodies" knew that the greater community would meet their physical needs, so they used this as an opportunity to do nothing.

One of the interesting questions of this text is found in trying to uncover what led to the situation in Thessalonica. Some biblical scholars suggest that it was nothing more than a few lazy church members who recognized an easy situation of which they could take advantage. Since these believers knew the community would take care of them, they were merely choosing not to take care of themselves.

Other scholars believe that the congregation's confusion and infatuation regarding the imminent return of Christ had helped to create this situation of laziness. Since these believers fully anticipated the return of Christ at any moment, they had simply given up on life and work. They were now spending their days waiting and watching the skies. This attitude has surfaced in the church at numerous times over the centuries. It has been particularly prevalent at points in history when apocalyptic enthusiasm and anticipation reached high levels. It certainly isn't difficult to believe that this could have been the situation in Thessalonica as well. After all, much of 1 and 2 Thessalonians is rooted in Paul's attempts to provide a proper theology of the Parousia, so it should not be surprising that these same issues were also responsible for this particular situation.

Active Christianity (2 Thess 3:6-13)

In this relatively short text, Paul employs familiar themes in the attempt to convey the importance of hard work. First, Paul points out that every believer plays an integral role in the well-being of the community. If we fail to work hard or do our part as individuals, the entire community will suffer.

First Corinthians 12 is arguably Paul's most familiar attempt to communicate this perspective. In that particular passage, Paul uses his classic example of the human body as an illustration of the significance of every member of the local church. Despite the fact that some parts of the body may appear more important than others, Paul demonstrates that all aspects of the human body must do their part in order for the body to function as it should. In the same way, regardless of one's apparent gifts or significance, everyone is essential to the well-being of the body of Christ.

I once preached a sermon in which each member of the congregation was given one piece of a large jigsaw puzzle. As I spoke about everyone's unique gifts and talents, I encouraged them to look at their puzzle pieces. As they did, I made a similar assertion that without the contribution of each piece, the puzzle could not be completed. I wanted them to recognize that all gifts function in a complementary way. If anyone fails to share his or her gift, the church will never be all God wants it to be. Each gift is essential to the success and progress of the kingdom.

Paul uses these verses from 2 Thessalonians to communicate the same message. Failure by any members of the Thessalonian church to pull their own weight would result in the effectiveness of the entire church being diminished. As an interconnected body, each and every member was absolutely essential to the well-being of all others. If any member decided to shirk responsibility, Paul wanted them to recognize that they were actually damaging the entire family of faith. After all, if this young congregation with limited resources cared for the needs of those who were idle, would they have enough left to provide for those with legitimate needs who sought help? (DeSilva, 74)

Second, Paul points to himself and his missionary companions in vv. 7 and following as examples of what it means to work hard and to pull one's own weight. In session 2 we dealt with 1 Thessalonians 2 and the controversy surrounding Paul's motives for spending time in Thessalonica. There we focused on the fact that Paul used his own life and actions in Thessalonica as a way of disputing the accusations levied against him. Here again, Paul holds himself up as an example of proper Christian living.

As has been stated elsewhere, Paul, Timothy, and Silas each paid their own way while in Thessalonica. Rather than taking payment from the Thessalonians, they plied their crafts and provided for their own needs. They demonstrated the importance of hard work and in no way insinuated through their own behavior that laziness was appropriate. While many believers today must offer the refrain "do as I say, not as I do," Paul was able to refer confidently to himself as someone to emulate. (Gaventa, 130)

One may also be struck by Paul's words in 2 Thessalonians 3:10. Paul shows his seriousness on the matter by clearly stating that those who do not work should not eat. These words may strike the modern reader as harsh, particularly in light of the importance believers today place on treating others with grace and love. Nonetheless, Paul's statement calls everyone who participates in community life to recognize that the church is in reality a two-way street. The church exists to meet our needs and to care for everyone. At the same time, however, the community has every right to anticipate and to expect each member to make his or her own unique contributions to the congregation's greater good. Reading Paul closely may mean coming to the conclusion that if we do not do our part, there may come a day when the church is no longer obligated to fulfill our expectations of the church.

Lessons from Thessalonians

It is commonly held that we live in a consumer-driven society. We often choose products and service providers based on what they can do for us. It is rare for us to have to make choices based on what an individual or group should *expect* from us. This characteristic of everyday life in modern America is also alive and well within the church. Today, many people want churches to meet their needs and live up to their high standards. Most people, however, give little thought or consideration to what the church should expect from them.

In light of modern expectations of excellence in all phases of programming from worship services to the church soccer league, a new attitude is needed. After all, sustaining such ministries necessitates deep and lasting commitment and involvement on the part of the entire church community. As a result, if today's church is to survive and thrive in the years ahead, we must move away from the axiom that "twenty percent of the people do eighty percent of the work" and adopt a guiding principle that expects all of the people to recognize that they are crucial to the congregation's well-being.

This shift is not only dependent on the laity. Such a transition also demands a concerted effort on behalf of clergy. While many ministers today are quick to lament a lack of congregational participation in sharing ministry responsibilities, most are just as likely to have difficulty turning over programs and decisions to their membership. Creating a culture of participation and servants requires a leadership team constantly willing to invite others to join them in their work. Such a culture also requires egos that are able to take a lesser role regularly so that others may occasionally seize the wheel.

Finally, leaders who call others to do their part must follow Paul by exhibiting hard work themselves. People will rarely be energized by someone who can merely say the right things. Today's church needs leaders who exemplify a servant attitude.

1. If you had been a part of the Thessalonian church, how would you have felt about idle members living off the graces of the congregation?

_____
_____
_____
_____
_____
_____

2. Do you feel that Paul was too harsh on those who were not working? Why or why not?

_____
_____
_____
_____
_____
_____

3. How do you feel about Paul's use of himself as an example? Was he being arrogant or simply exhibiting leadership?

_____
_____
_____
_____
_____
_____

4. What percentage of your congregation serves in some capacity? What factors let you to this answer?

_____
_____
_____
_____
_____

5 Does your church's leadership team do a good job of encouraging and inviting others to get involved in the congregation's work? If yes, how? If not, why not?

_____

_____

_____

_____

_____

_____

6. How does one balance the amount of time spent serving with the amount of time spent taking advantage of the church's ministries?

_____

_____

_____

_____

_____

_____

7. Have you ever experienced "buffet Christianity"? In what ways is this form of church involvement common in your particular community?

_____

_____

_____

_____

_____

_____

Live Actively—Work

Live as Family—Discipline

2 Thessalonians 3:14-15

Central Truth of the Session

Christians do not always live according to the commands of the New Testament. There is nothing new about this reality. If one reads the New Testament carefully, he or she will discover countless situations in which Jesus' followers did not act in Christlike ways. In the Thessalonian correspondence, guidelines for proper behavior assume the presence of disobedience. In light of these moral lapses, Paul is clear that those who disobey should be disciplined.

This is a point at which many modern congregations diverge from their spiritual ancestors. While we definitely continue to wrestle with regular disobedience in the modern church, discipline is a rare occurrence. Christians often say that they want the twenty-first-century church to be characterized by love and grace, yet our failure to exhibit discipline may be one of the most unloving things we do. This session will explore discipline in both the Thessalonian congregation and modern failures to provide loving correction within the church.

The Intersection of Thessalonians and Today

During high school I entered a period in which I was more interested in watching television than studying. As you might guess, my grades quickly suffered. When report cards came out and my parents became aware of my educational laziness, I was grounded as punishment. Until my grades improved, I wasn't allowed to watch television on school nights, and my extracurricular activities were significantly curtailed.

Obviously, as a teenager, these restrictions were not easy for me to handle. My perspective at the time was that my parents were being too harsh. Looking back on that experience, I now recognize that my parents were actually responding properly and out of love. They realized that I was at a critical point in my academic career. They wanted me to excel in school and to prepare adequately for the rigors of college that were just around the bend. This desire led my mom and dad to discipline me. My parents knew I wouldn't like their decision, but they also recognized that their actions were in my best interests.

In the focal passage for this session, Paul calls for believers in Thessalonica to make a tough decision regarding those in the congregation who are acting inappropriately. In the text, the apostle calls for the disobedient believers to be banished from the community for a period of time. From the early church forward, there have been people who felt Paul was too harsh in his indictment and punishment of straying believers. In reality, Paul, like my parents, was actually motivated by love and care. The intention was not for the disobedient believers to remain ostracized from the community forever. Instead, Paul hoped that through the congregation's strong stance, those in the wrong would learn from their mistakes, grow from the experience, and return to the community even more committed than they had been previously.

The Thessalonian Context

Although this session focuses exclusively on vv. 14 and 15, it is important to recognize that these words are intimately connected to those that come before them in 2 Thessalonians 3. Paul's call for discipline is related to the situation in which members of the congregation had stopped working and were choosing to spend each day living idly. Except, that is, for laboring diligently to keep up with other people's business!

In v. 10, Paul goes so far as to say that the community sluggards shouldn't eat if they refuse to work. In vv. 14 and 15, the expressed attitude takes things one step further as the apostle says that refusal to work should also result in at least temporary banishment from the community. There should be no doubt that Paul saw these offenses as serious. Those choosing not to work were manipulating the system and preying on the church's commitment to care for and support one another. Perhaps even more importantly, the "lazy bones" were also draining the church's coffers, which might ultimately prevent the congregation from appropriately responding to genuine community needs in the future.

It is also important to recognize that the necessity of discipline in the Thessalonian context was far different than in our modern Christian culture. This issue had to be handled carefully. If the situation was not tended to with care, permanent damage could have resulted in the faith lives of either those in the wrong or those being wronged within the Thessalonian church. Unlike today, there were no other options available to the Thessalonians for church involvement except this small community founded by Paul.

Think about it: today, if we are not pleased with the decisions our local congregation makes, we may ultimately choose to involve ourselves with another body of believers. In Thessalonica, there were no other choices. If those who were lazy felt they had been signaled out and disciplined too harshly by Paul, they had one choice. They could leave the church altogether. Likewise, those who were committed to the church and felt they were being taken advantage of had no options either. (Wright, 160)

Tough Love (2 Thess 3:14-15)

One of the important things to recognize here is Paul's use of the word "family" to describe the Thessalonian community. As mentioned in other parts of this study, Paul understood the function of a family to be one of the best metaphors for the way members of a congregation should relate to one another. Certainly one can get wrapped up in the no-nonsense approach that the apostle takes in his response to the problematic situation in Thessalonica. Yet, a close reading makes it obvious that everything Paul says was peppered with an attitude of love and ultimate redemption.

In light of this, it becomes easy to see how vv. 14 and 15 balance one another in Paul's attempt to exhibit and advocate tough love. In v. 14, Paul's attitude is stern and to the point. Those who are lazy should get back to work. It was time for them to stop taking advantage of the generosity of others. If the idle believers continued to flaunt their laziness, the congregation had no choice but to cut them off from the community.

Verse 15 follows the tough words of v. 14 with the balance of compassion. Just as Paul wanted to be clear about what needed to take place in order to right the ship in Thessalonica, he also hoped everyone would recognize the real motivation behind this stern stance. If anyone had to be exiled from the community for a time, they were not to be treated as enemies; rather, they were to be treated as family. This statement is rich with the anticipation that the temporary community banishment would result in redemption and reentry into the family.

When reading this text, it is also interesting to take note of the punishment Paul suggests. He doesn't infer that those in the wrong should be beaten or given a good tongue-lashing. Instead, Paul advocates temporary isolation. The wise apostle understood that life together was one of the most treasured aspects of any community of faith. When taken away, it was likely to be missed.

Things haven't changed much over the centuries. It could be said that the communal aspect of the Christian life remains one of the most beloved aspects of faith for modern believers. In a world where it is so easy to live anonymously, it is refreshing to enter a group that knows each other by name and that accepts everyone unconditionally. Journeying through each day with others who are ready to support, care, and listen is the greatest way to live.

My family sees this fact played out regularly in our own home. When our preschool-aged daughter gets into trouble, there is one mode of punishment she despises more than all the others. She hates to be sent to her room. Why? For her, being removed from the rest of the family and forced to be alone for even a short period of time is almost unbearable.

We may think this is merely a child's response, but the truth is that few of us enjoy time spent in isolation. If Paul were to advise us on how to provide discipline within the context of church life today, it seems plausible to assume that he would choose the same method recommended to the Thessalonians.

Lessons from Thessalonians

Exerting discipline within today's church requires a great deal of courage. In fact, many ministers might suggest that the decision to discipline could cause more damage than good. Even when discipline seems to be the absolute right path to take, many view such actions as judgmental and thus inappropriate. Further still, one never knows how someone in need of correction will respond to the suggestion, much less their friends or family. These realities have led many church leaders to abandon any thoughts of discipline and effectively to "sweep problems under the rug."

While such an attitude may keep the peace, this stance is a difficult one to take in light of Paul's teaching that the church should function as a family. As has already been stated, we all appreciate the fact that authentic family relationships sometimes require brutal honesty and difficult decisions. In such occasions, the critical attitudes are love and care. Tough decisions and honest words must always have in mind the best interests of the person being disciplined. The intent is to help them, never to harm them.

It is also important to recognize that even though a failure to discipline may result in momentary peace, it could be ultimately detrimental to the person in need of correction. For instance, our children may love the idea of staying up until midnight watching television on a school night; however, the next day their academic astuteness and ability will likely be nonexistent. This reality makes doing the truly loving things a simple decision.

Unfortunately, we often fail to carry this type of familial common sense into the day-to-day affairs of the church. Life is hectic, demanding, and uncertain in most of today's congregations. The idea of momentary peace seems like such a precious commodity that few churches seem willing to utilize New Testament discipline in any form. In turn, issues go unresolved, problems go unfixed, and church members are sometimes allowed to continue to act however they please. In light of this, Paul might judge most modern congregations to be heavy on peace but light on love.

Beyond avoidance, another major issue for churches is failure to discipline in a spirit of love. When we do gain the courage to speak honestly with members about an issue or suggest some type of course correction, we often approach the guilty party as an enemy rather than a friend. Even in the church, tempers flare, hateful words are spoken, and long-term friendships can quickly erode. Despite the fact that disappointing behavior leads to discipline, Paul reminds us in v. 15 that the perpetrator is a brother or sister in Christ and not an enemy.

We must also approach all such issues with redemption as our ultimate goal. As was the case in Thessalonica, punishment is only a means toward the end of renewed and redeemed involvement in the community. As a family, our ultimate hope is always for every brother and sister to occupy their chair at the table.

I have a close friend who was doing genealogical research and discovered a story about his great-great-grandfather being threatened with discipline by his church in the early 1800s. Evidently this man had a son whose horse had gotten loose and knocked down a fellow church member's fence, causing damage to his wheat. The grandfather had tried to make amends, but not to the satisfaction of the neighbor. Believe it or not, as the disagreement lingered, the congregational board became involved and threatened to bar both parties from the Communion table unless they resolved their differences and made peace.

The records show that the church board met with the involved parties several times and evidently considered the issue a serious matter. While today's congregations would likely never get involved in such a dispute, this congregation's leadership made it clear that peace and civility were not only concepts they talked about. These were also ideas that the congregation expected its members to embody through their actions, particularly within church family relationships.

Discipline is never an easy thing to do. Such a decision always requires much prayer, deep thinking, and carefully planned actions. Nonetheless, a willingness to be honest with others when we sense that they are in the wrong is at the heart of the Christian message. It is one of the painful yet necessary ways that God works in all our lives to shape us into the people God desires us to be.

1. How comfortable are you with the idea of discipline within the local church? If this idea makes you uncomfortable, why?

_____

_____

_____

_____

_____

_____

2. Have you ever been part of a congregation that needed to discipline someone and failed to do so? If so, describe the situation.

_____

_____

_____

_____

_____

_____

3. Have you ever been part of a congregation that chose to discipline someone? How was the decision received?

_____

_____

_____

_____

_____

_____

4. How can we properly balance love, grace, and discipline within the modern church?

_____

_____

_____

_____

_____

_____

5. What roles do honest speech and discipline play within your family?

_____

_____

_____

_____

_____

_____

6. Do you agree with this session's suggestion that keeping the peace is one of the primary reasons church discipline is so rare today? Why or why not? What are other reasons for the avoidance of discipline in the local churches today?

_____

_____

_____

_____

_____

_____

Live as Family—Discipline

7. In what ways are we failing one another when we do not provide discipline in the local church?

_____

_____

_____

_____

_____

_____

8. In what other ways does the modern church fail to function as a family?

_____

_____

_____

_____

_____

_____

9. Are there ways that the church disciplines today that are similar to yet different from Paul's apprach? If so, how?

_____

_____

_____

_____

_____

_____

10. Was there a heightened need for discipline in the Thessalonian context? If so, why?

_____

_____

_____

_____

_____

_____

Bibliography

Barclay, William. *The Letters to the Philippians, Colossians, and Thessalonians,* Daily Bible Study Series, revised edition. Louisville: Westminister John Knox, 1975.

Biema, David Van, and Jeff Chu. "Does God Want You to Be Rich," *Time* 168/12 (16 September 2006).

Blevins, James L. "Letters to the Thessalonians," in *Mercer Dictionary of the Bible,* ed. Watson E. Mills et al. Macon GA: Mercer University Press, 1990.

Bonhoeffer, Dietrich. *The Cost of Discipleship.* Revised edition. New York: McMillan, 1970.

Calvin, John. *1 & 2 Thessalonians, The Crossway Classic Commentaries,* ed. Alister McGrath and J. I. Packer. Wheaton IL & Nottingham, England: Crossway Books, 1999.

DeSilva, David A. *Paul and the Macedonians: The Life and Letters of Paul.* Nashville: Abingdon Press, 2001.

Efird, James M. *The New Testament Writings: History, Literature, Interpretation.* Louisville: John Knox, 1980.

Ehrman, Bart. *Peter, Paul & Mary Magdalene: The Followers of Jesus in History and Legend.* New York: Oxford Press, 2006.

Gaventa, Beverly Roberts. *First and Second Thessalonians.* Interpretation: A Bible Commentary for Teaching and Preaching, ed. James Luther Mays. Louisville: John Knox, 1998.

Hendrix, John D. *To Thessalonians with Love.* Nashville: Broadman Press, 1982.

Hobbs, Herschel H., et al. *Commentary of 1–2 Thessalonians. The Broadman Bible Commentary Series,* vol. 11, ed. Clifton J. Allen. Nashville: Broadman, 1971.

Hybels, Bill, and Mark Mittelberg. *Becoming a Contagious Christian.* Grand Rapids MI: Zondervan, 1994.

Jordan, Clarence. *The Cotton Patch Version of Paul's Epistles.* Clinton NJ: New Win Publishing, 1968.

Miller, Calvin. "Relational Evangelism." Preached at Johns Creek Baptist Church. Alpharetta GA. 17 September 2006.

Murphy-O'Connor, Jerome. *Paul His Story.* Oxford: Oxford University Press, 2004.

Smith, Abraham, et al. *First and Second Letters to the Thessalonians.* The New Interpreter's Bible Commentary, vol. 11. Nashville: Abingdon Press, 2000.

Tolbert, Malcolm O. *Philippians, Colossians, 1 & 2 Thessalonians, 1& 2 Timothy, Tutus, Philemon. Layman's Bible Book Commentary,* vol. 22. Nashville: Broadman Press, 1980.

Wright, Tom. *Paul for Everyone: Galatians and Thessalonians.* Louisville: Westminster John Knox, 2004.

———. *Simply Christian.* New York: HarperCollins, 2006.